طفل الشاطئ

THE BOY
ON THE
BEACH

My Family's Escape from Syria and
Our Hope for a New Home

TIMA KURDI

PUBLISHED BY SIMON & SCHUSTER

NEW YORK   LONDON   TORONTO   SYDNEY   NEW DELHI

SIMON &
SCHUSTER
CANADA

Simon & Schuster Canada
A Division of Simon & Schuster, Inc.
166 King Street East, Suite 300
Toronto, Ontario M5A 1J3

This Simon & Schuster Canada edition April 2018

SIMON & SCHUSTER CANADA and colophon are trademarks of Simon & Schuster, Inc.

For information about special discounts for bulk purchases, please contact Simon & Schuster Special Sales at 1-800-268-3216 or CustomerService@simonandschuster.ca.

Library and Archives Canada Cataloguing in Publication

Kurdi, Tima, author
    The boy on the beach : my family's escape from Syria and
our hope for a new home / Tima Kurdi.
Issued in print and electronic formats
ISBN 978-1-5011-7523-7 (hardcover). —ISBN 978-1-5011-7525-1 (ebook)

    1. Kurdi, Tima.   2. Syrian Canadians—Biography.
3. Immigrants—Canada—Biography.   4. Kurdi, Alan, 2012–2015—Family.
5. Syria—History—Civil War, 2011—Refugees.   I. Title.
FC106.S98Z7 2017   971004'92756910092   C2017-904189-4
                                                   C2017-904190-8

Manufactured in the United States of America

10   9   8   7   6   5   4   3

ISBN 978-1-5011-7523-7
ISBN 978-1-5011-7525-1 (ebook)

To Abdullah,
for his courage in sharing his story.

To my baba,
for giving our family the strength to go on and to never lose hope.

It's like a flower
He doesn't have water
He die
Come to Canada
He has water
And opens up again
—SHERGO KURDI

Alan Kurdi (*left*) and Ghalib Kurdi (*right*)
Rest in peace, angels.

Contents

CONTENTS

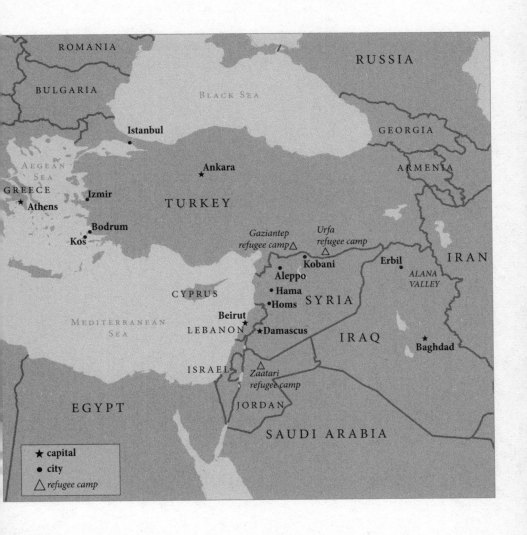

The family of
Ghalib and Radiya Kurdi

Ghalib KURDI
m. **Radiya**

Mohammad
m. Ghouson
- **Heveen**
- **Shergo**
- **Ranim**
- **Rezan**
- **Sherwan**

Tima
(1) m. Sirwan —— **Alan**
(2) m. Rocco

Maha
m. Ghalib
- **Rodeen**
- **Adnan**
- **Barehan**
- **Fatima**
- **Mahmoud**
- **Yasmeen**
- **Mohammad**
- **Shireen**

Abdullah
m. Rehanna
- **Ghalib**
- **Alan**

Shireen
m. Lowee
- **Yasser**
- **Farzat**
- **Maleek**

Hivron
m. Ahmad
- **Rawan**
- **Abdulrahman**
- **Ghoufran**
- **Noor**
- **Maya**

Preface

I can see it from here," said my brother, Abdullah, describing the land-scape to me, his older sister, far away and safe in my home in Canada. "It's right there," he said. "So close and yet so far."

My brother was a refugee fleeing Syria, standing on Turkish soil and looking at Kos, a large, soft-shouldered Greek island on the horizon. During the day, Kos was a mirage in the middle distance. At night it twinkled with life and seemed close enough to touch. For thousands of Syrian refugees during the summer of 2015, that island shimmering across the sea was their touchstone, their last hope for a better future.

"One hundred per cent, the smuggler said, we'll go tomorrow," Abdullah texted me.

"Talk to Dad before you leave," I texted back.

Thunderstorms rolled in and out, pushed by high winds of as much as eighty kilometres per hour, delaying their departure. A few days passed.

August 9: "Leaving tonight." But there were more thunderstorms and gusty winds.

August 10: "We went, but the smuggler sent us back."

"Did you lose your money?" I texted.

"No. We will try again tonight. Don't worry, sister, go to sleep."

It was impossible not to worry. Each time Abdullah texted, "We're leaving tonight," I held my breath. There is an eight-hour time difference between Turkey and my home in Vancouver, Canada, and I got into the habit of going to sleep early so that I could wake up before dawn to check my cellphone. But my husband had to keep regular working hours, and so, to preserve his sanity, I left my cellphone in the kitchen every night. Every morning, the butterflies knocking in my stomach would wake me up, and I would rush to the kitchen for my phone. Every day for a month, each time that phone made a peep, my heart threw a fit.

My brother was only four kilometres from the shores of Kos, *so close and yet so far*. He was living in Bodrum, Turkey. He had escaped Syria and the terrorist groups that had overtaken our homeland. He and his family had survived many hardships in Istanbul as poor illegal immigrants, barely able to keep themselves fed and housed. They had endured the callous indifference of the many governments that had closed their doors to them. Turkey now offered the closest available corridor to Greece, the only country in the region from which refugees could get to the few northern European countries accepting Syrian refugees. Countries where life was a bit better. In Germany and Sweden, for instance, refugees were offered legal asylum and resettlement, something Turkey and many other neighbouring countries in the Middle East did not provide. And refugee children could go to school, something they could not do in Turkey.

But reaching that Greek Island was no easy feat. First Abdullah had to get his wife, Rehanna, and their two young sons, Ghalib and Alan, across the Aegean Sea, across a patch of the Mediterranean monitored by police and coast guard officials ready to turn the refugees back to the shore. This was a stretch of sea known for its late summer winds, which can materialize in an instant and blow for days, turning the water into a rabid beast. Abdullah had to believe that he could get his family safely across that passage. They had crossed vast swaths of dangerous terrain to reach Turkey. Surely they could make it across four more kilometres to find hope for a new life on the other side.

To make that crossing, Abdullah had to trust smugglers. His family could not make the crossing legally via the many large ferries that criss-cross the sea, because the Turkish authorities required valid documentation to exit the country, and legal entry to the majority of European countries, including Greece, required valid passports and visas, with a long list of requirements that only wealthy Syrians could meet—bank statements, insurance, passport photos. Abdullah, like most refugees, had a passport, but after so many years of war, it had expired; his wife and young sons had never had passports. The smugglers provided space on boats, for a fee. But even the highest amounts didn't satisfy the smugglers' greed, and they typically overloaded the boats far beyond safe capacity for maximum profit.

That year, close to one million refugees had arrived in Europe by sea, and the lion's share of those desperate souls were Syrians landing in Greece. By June, the Greek coast guard had rescued almost fifty thousand people, but thousands more drowned in the Mediterranean. As many as one in four of them were children, the majority under the age of twelve. Five per cent were infants.

My nephew Ghalib had recently turned four and his little brother, Alan, was just twenty-seven months old when their desperate parents took that perilous journey on a raft to seek a better life. You must be

wondering, "What could possibly compel refugees to make that dangerous crossing, risking their lives and those of their children?" It may be
impossible to comprehend unless you've lived the life of a refugee.

At that time, four of my five siblings and their families had escaped
to Turkey, barely able to keep their young families afloat. By the summer
of 2015, with the Syrian war in its fifth year and no end in sight, their
situations had become more desperate. Many of my siblings, my nieces
and nephews, my cousins, and other relatives were poised to risk that
crossing; a few of them had already made it all the way to Germany and
Sweden, where conditions were better. All my siblings had young children, and with no access to school, the kids were falling behind; many
of my teenaged nieces and nephews had to work in Turkish sweatshops
to help their parents make ends meet. My younger brother, Abdullah,
did not want the same fate for his two boys. His hopes for them were
simple—adequate food and shelter, education, and health care—but ful-
filling those basic needs was impossible in Syria and beyond challenging
in Turkey.

I knew all too well the kind of life that my brothers and sisters had
endured since their families had been forced to flee Damascus in 2012.
I had seen for myself their destitute living situation in Istanbul when I
visited in 2014. That's when I started saving money to help my family get
out of Turkey. At first I went through official channels, trying to provide
them a safe harbour in Canada. My husband and I had committed to
privately sponsoring my eldest brother Mohammad's family, and we had
also started collecting the application paperwork for Abdullah's sponsorship. But my attempts failed. I couldn't get all the paperwork needed—it
was impossible to get documents from a country destroyed by war—and
the price of two private applications at once was just too much. By the
summer of 2015, I had given up hope of Canadian asylum for Abdullah and his family. I decided to give him five thousand dollars to pay

the smuggler's demand for him, his wife, and my two little nephews. Of course, I had many, many doubts about whether I should do this. But in times of such abject desperation, knowing that my family was already in such danger, I decided to pay for the journey. There isn't a day that goes by when I wish I hadn't. There isn't a day that goes by when I don't wish for my beautiful sister-in-law and my sweet nephews to be with us still.

At the end of July, Abdullah texted me from Istanbul: "I got the money. Your friends are nice people." He had received the last chunk of the smuggler's fee. The next day, he and his family departed for Izmir, a port city about halfway between Istanbul and Bodrum and a hub for refugees to meet smugglers. The refugees were easy to find. Thousands of them camped overnight in parks. And they would often share their smuggler contacts.

Abdullah secured a smuggler in Izmir and talked to other refugees about their experiences. Many of them had scary stories about attempted crossings on those flimsy rubber dinghies. Abdullah and Rehanna were petrified by the thought of getting on a dinghy; they wanted a sturdy fiberglass boat, but the smuggler repeatedly told him they couldn't afford that. They could afford good life jackets. But those weren't easy to find. I had heard news of refugees who drowned after their life jackets became waterlogged and heavy. There were many fake life jackets on the market. Abdullah called me while he was shopping.

"How can you tell the difference between the real ones and the fakes?" he asked.

"I don't know. Buy the most expensive ones. How are the kids?"

"They have colds. And Alan is teething. I bought some hard biscuits for him."

I remember every call he made to me, every message he left me during this time. I still have every text he sent. That long chain of messages provides a record of the events that transpired. It is also a testament to the human condition under extreme pressure, to our hopes and fears, to our many nagging doubts and anxieties—about the impending voyage and so much more than that, going right back to our earliest memories of ourselves.

August 11: "Didn't go."

As the days inched by and Abdullah refused to take a rubber dinghy, my anxiety turned to frustration, and I pushed him to just make the journey or call it quits and return to Istanbul. Later, reading back through my texts, I could hear the voice of a nagging older sister, prodding her younger brother: stay put, turn back, be more cautious, be less cautious, just get it done.

I put so much pressure on Abdullah that he sent me a video of the sea. Those big waves filled me with dread.

August 21: "The waves were too high. I would not do it."

The next morning, I texted him again. "Where are you? What's going on?"

"On the street. The waves were too big again last night. If the boss smuggler tells his men not to go, that's it, they won't go."

August 25: "We're going tonight." The weather was perfect. They got all the way to the point. The smugglers arrived. But there were at least forty other refugees being herded into the boat. Abdullah refused to board.

August 27: "Water so calm today. But the smugglers had a rubber dinghy. I won't take a rubber dinghy."

That night: "The water is peaceful. Rehanna's heart and my heart say tomorrow." I called him as soon as I received that text. It was already the morning of August 28 in Turkey. Alan was laughing in the background, as usual; that boy was always laughing. But Ghalib was worried. He said, "Auntie, I just phoned Baba Shikho"—that's what Ghalib called his grandfather, Rehanna's father—"I told him I want to go back to my bedroom with my toys. Baba said they're still there. I asked him to please bring the truck and take me home."

Imagine being a grandparent on the receiving end of that call. How might you explain to two tiny boys that home is now gone, that it will never return to the way it was before? As for Alan, he was so young that he had yet to start speaking in sentences. Aside from pointing—to a banana, a stuffed toy, a sailboat on the horizon—he could not even communicate his hopes and dreams. To get his dad's attention, Alan would cup Abdullah's face so that their eyes locked. And then he would smile, or laugh, or stick out his tongue. In those incredibly stressful days, it was as if he were saying, "Smile, Baba. Everything will be okay."

Many of Abdullah's texts contained similar comforts to us. In hindsight, I wonder if he was trying to reassure himself that the basic freedoms and dignities of life were within reach, that home, even a temporary one, was an attainable place.

The following morning, I woke up to another short text: "Didn't leave."

When Abdullah sent me another message—"...إن شاء الله, *Inshallah*. God willing, we're leaving tonight."—I admit that I expected to wake up the next morning to another "Didn't leave."

August 31: There were no messages from Abdullah. That long chain of texts ends with at least a half-dozen texts from me, asking, "Where are you?" "What happened?" "Text me, please."

All my messages were sent to the bottom of the Mediterranean Sea.

Rehanna, Ghalib, and Alan Kurdi all drowned in the Mediterranean Sea on September 2, 2015. Since the tragedy, I have asked, "Why them? Why us?" thousands of times, as many times as refugees have drowned in the

Mediterranean Sea. At other moments, I have lashed out far and wide, in every direction. I have cried out to the governments that have denied a safe harbour to so many refugees, or failed to provide a slip of paper that legitimizes their right to the most basic necessities. I have asked the military forces, the rebel fighters, and the ISIS terrorists that have turned our homelands in Damascus and Kobani into rivers of blood, "Why? What are you fighting for? Oil? Political ideologies? Religion? Power? Revenge?" I have called out to the global authorities, in the Middle East, Western Europe, America, and Canada, "We are not animals. We are human beings, just like you. Why did you close your hearts and minds to forging a peaceful end to this war?" Still other times, I have shouted at the smugglers and human traffickers, the faceless boogeymen who have profited from misery: "Why is money more important to you than human life?"

I have often envisioned the island of Kos, the stable rocks of the cradle of Western Civilization that my brothers and sisters could see from the shores of Bodrum. Such a short journey, four kilometres. Why couldn't that island have been just a little closer? I have asked the sea and the wind, "Why did you take our loved ones from us?" I have called out to the media, "Why did you ignore the plight of the refugees for so long? Until it was too late to save my nephews and sister-in-law? And why did some of you attack Abdullah's reputation, after he'd lost everything else?" Often, I have cried to God, "Why?" Sometimes he didn't answer. Sometimes he responded with a question of his own. Sometimes I knew how to answer it. Other times, I was speechless.

I have reserved the most vicious condemnations for myself. I may appear to be an average middle-aged woman going about my business, shopping for groceries, cooking a meal for my family, resting my head on a pillow at the end of the day. My body is there, going through the motions, but my mind is somewhere else. In a brightly lit interrogation room, staring myself down across the table, demanding, "Why did you send Abdullah that money for the smugglers? Why didn't you send him more money, so that he could take a safer, seaworthy boat? Why didn't you go to Bodrum and rent a motorboat, like so many tourists and holiday-makers, and take your family across the sea? Why didn't you start trying to get your family to Canada on the very first day that the war in Syria started? Why were you so foolish and naive? So selfish?" I'm still lost at sea, drifting. Sometimes I float. Other times I sink like a stone and drown.

At some point before the tragedy, my family began living on borrowed time. When did it start? How long ago? When ISIS began to put a chokehold on my ancestral homeland? Years before, when Rehanna was pregnant with Ghalib and the first rumblings of protest against the Syrian government began? Decades earlier, after I emigrated to Canada as a young woman? Before I was born?

When you wake up from a nightmare, you reach out to your loved ones, seeking solace, warmth, and safety. Among my family, we often discussed our waking nightmare, and those conversations steered us back in time, to memories from the past, our family's past, our people's past. About what life was like *before*. Perhaps we were attempting to find a place where we could truly belong, whether it was a place we'd already lived or somewhere else. A man-made disaster forced us to abandon our homeland, but there was at least some comfort in knowing that we carried our history deep within us.

When I began to write this book in August 2016, a month shy of the anniversary of the tragedy, Abdullah was in the intensive care unit of a Turkish hospital, clinging to life. In his hospital bed, he often slipped into delirium, calling for his wife and his boys—"I need to get them clothes, water, and food"—as if he were still preparing them for the journey. The doctors told me he needed heart surgery and that there was an eighty per cent chance that he would die. When my father heard the news, he said, "I would gladly give my son my heart." Then my father too had to be rushed to the hospital in Damascus. My father didn't want to worry me, so I didn't know what was wrong with him exactly, but I believed the true cause of his illness was heartbreak.

Even in my deepest moments of despair, I recognized that we were the lucky ones: we, the living. We had lost too many loved ones and nothing would bring them back, but we were alive. We had our memories and our cognizance. We had many wonderful children and grandchildren with whom we could share our history. It was our honour and our duty to pass those memories to the next generation, to put words on paper and share them, not just with our relatives but also with the world. By writing this book, I was attempting to document the story of Abdullah's family—to give it a permanence that wouldn't otherwise exist.

"Millions of refugees are in the same desperate situation as us," Abdullah said to me every time I pushed him for more information. But his story bears witness to the experiences of millions of refugees and the many victims of war and genocide around the world.

When you saw the photograph of that little boy, my dear nephew Alan, dead on a faraway shore, you became a part of our family. You shared our horror, our heartache, our shock, and our outrage. You wanted to save him, but you knew it was too late. In your grief, you reached out, and by doing so, you grabbed hold of my hand and pulled me to you. You joined my family's chorus of grief. You helped save me from drowning.

I hope that my words help bring all of us one step closer to each other. I hope that my story, tragic as it is, also plants the seed of hope in your hearts and minds. I hope it inspires you to join me in speaking up for all the people who have no voice. And for all the children who were taken from us before they could speak.

In Syria and other Arab countries, we call elders "auntie" and "uncle"—strangers, friends, and family alike. If you are older than me, you are my aunties and uncles, and if you are younger than me, I am your auntie. Now our histories and our destinies are entwined. Now we are all one family.

THE BOY
ON THE
BEACH

PART

ONE

ياسمين الشام

Yāsmīn al-Sham

The City of Jasmine

In Damascus, jasmine grows wild everywhere and seems to spring out of every vacant nook and cranny so that the air is permeated with its sweet smell. There is so much jasmine in Damascus that the city is nicknamed ياسمين الشام, *Yāsmīn al-Sham*, or the City of Jasmine.

I have made many attempts to grow *yāsmīn* in my garden in Vancouver, Canada, but the flowers never give off much of a scent. My father even shipped me a bulb from my birthplace of Damascus, which all the locals simply call Sham. In the spring, I planted that bulb in the garden, and it blossomed that summer, but you had to stick your nose right inside the petals to get a subtle whiff of its hypnotic scent. That bulb survived away from home soil for one winter, but it didn't survive the next.

I was safe in Canada, where I'd lived since 1992, when half a world away, my family was forced to leave their homeland after war erupted in Syria in 2011. Like that bulb, they had to grow new roots in foreign soil. And the conditions they had to survive in were far from ideal. It is often said that to understand where you're going, you have to first understand where you've been. Before I give you the details of my siblings' tumultuous lives since they fled Syria, I want to tell you where we came from and what life was like before.

My father, غالب, Ghalib, was born in 1942, just before the dawn of a new era for much of the world, including Syria, which had been under the thumb of many different rulers for a few thousand years. My father was born in Hama. Ethnically, he is Kurdish. Like the majority of Syrians, many Kurds are Sunni Muslim, though they are known as the most religiously diverse culture in the world because they practice a mix of religious beliefs, and because their region straddles the many diverse cultures of Syria, Turkey, Iraq, and Iran. Like many Syrians in Hama, Ghalib's father (my grandfather) worked as a peasant farmer and my grandparents were poor. By the time my *baba* was born, the family already had two daughters and two sons. When my father was three years old, his mother died. We have a saying in Syria: "When the mother is gone, the family falls apart." My grandfather tried his best to take care of his children in between long hours working in the fields. But the young boys were often hungry and dirty, and their clothes were threadbare, until the neighbourhood women took those boys under their wings and provided them with food, shoes, clothes, and a place to shower occasionally.

When my father was six years old, his father moved the family to كوباني, Kobani, where my dad's family owned land. Kobani is a fertile region near the Turkish border, east of the Nahr Al Furat, the mighty Euphrates River. My grandfather had a plot of land on which he grew bulgur wheat, and the family lived in a one-room house of mud and hay. It was a typical agrarian life. While survival was a struggle at first,

4

especially because the boys had no mother to take care of them, my *baba* and his siblings relied on the kindness of their relatives and neighbours who grew enough food to eat and survive the winter months. When my father accompanied his older brother, Khalid, to graze the family's sheep, he also sampled the local wild herbs, grasses, and plants. My *baba* soon became an expert on which plants and herbs would make you ill and which ones could soothe a sick stomach.

To this day, my *baba* holds fast to a vivid memory of one such foraging excursion. After roaming the hillsides all day, he returned to the village, his belly rumbling. He discovered some watermelon rinds at the side of the road and he started to eat them. "Kids don't think about what they're eating, they just eat it," Baba said. A neighbour tending her vegetable garden yelled, "Don't eat that!" She plucked a plump tomato from her vine, came over to my father, and handed it to him. "Eat this instead," she said. It was dense in my father's palm and still warm from the summer sunshine. He bit into that tomato, and it was so ripe that its juices exploded in his mouth and ran down his chin. He still talks about that wonderful tomato, closing his eyes to reimagine its vibrant colour and to savour its warmth and taste. My father has eaten thousands of tomatoes since, but never has he enjoyed a tomato as much, because that tomato was flavoured with human kindness. That charitable act became firmly planted in my father's mind and heart, and he always passed along its lesson to his children. "You don't have to be rich with money to help others," he said, when I was growing up. "You just have to have a heart."

When my dad was a teenager, he left Kobani and returned to Hama to work. Soon after, he did his mandatory two-year conscription period with the Syrian military. Just as my dad's military stint was ending, he came down with malaria and had to be rushed to a hospital in Damascus. It was there that he met my mother, راضية, Radiya. My father claims that when my mom walked into that hospital room, it was love at first sight, and I believe it. When my father got out of the hospital, he went to stay with Radiya's relatives, and while he was there, my starry-eyed, lovestruck parents began their romance. My father got better, and soon the couple were desperate to be married.

After the wedding, the newlyweds continued to live in my mother's parents' house, while they saved to buy their own place. Their first son, my brother محمد, Mohammad, was born in 1968. A first-born son is considered a good fortune in many societies, and that is especially true of Arabic cultures. The eldest son has the greatest privileges as heir apparent, and everyone in the family, including the father, is identified by the first son's name. For example: my father is called أبو محمد, Abu Mohammad, meaning "the father of Mohammad," and my mother is أم محمد, Oum Mohammad, meaning "the mother of Mohammad." The first son's name also serves as a home address, so that if I gave you directions to my childhood home, I would tell you how to get to "the house of the father of Mohammad Kurdi." The eldest son also has the weightiest responsibilities: to respect and take care of his parents (especially when they are elderly) and his siblings, in particular his sisters—whether the sisters like it or not.

Soon after Mohammad's birth, both my mother's parents died. My mother's two older sisters were already married, but suddenly five of her six brothers, ranging from a four-year-old to teenaged boys, were orphans. My parents immediately took these children under their wing and treated them as their own. My dad saved his money after that and pooled it with money earned by my mom's teenaged brothers. In 1969, my parents bought a house in Rukn al-Din. Not just any house—it was the highest house on Mount Qasioun. My parents would often banter back and forth about our house's location. My dad would say, "I got you a top-notch house," to which my mom would reply, "It's going to give me a heart attack." But aside from its mountaintop location, it was a typical Syrian one-storey, with three bedrooms, a small kitchen, and a bathroom, made of concrete brick, with an open courtyard in the front, a little garden in the back, and a flat concrete roof.

In 1970, I was born. My parents named me فاطمة, Fatima; in Arabic it's pronounced "Fatmeh." The title of eldest daughter, much like eldest son, comes with its benefits and challenges. As the first daughter, I would be responsible for the household chores and for delegating those chores to all the younger sisters.

I did not have to wait long for helpers. My sister مها, Maha, was born in 1973. We were very different. Maha was quiet and shy, and a keen student; she loved to study. I preferred to be outside, playing marbles, skipping rope with the neighbourhood kids, and picking jasmine flowers with my friends, flowers which I would stitch together to make necklaces. When I was called inside to do homework, I'd stare out the window at the splendid view of Al Sham, neglecting the contents of my textbooks and pressing my jasmine blossoms between their pages so that they smelled divine.

From an early age, I wanted to be a *coiffereh*, a hairdresser. I performed my first haircut on a large, lifelike doll with blue eyes and long blond hair, which Maha and I shared. Very long hair was the fashion among Syrian girls. My own long hair was a nuisance, and maybe I was projecting my own wishful thinking when I cut that doll's hair very short. I loved its modern look, though Maha didn't and bawled her head off when she saw what I'd done.

My relationship with Mohammad was a different story. He and I were the first-born son and daughter, and maybe because of that, we argued a lot—so much that our parents nicknamed us Tom and Jerry, after the cartoon characters popular on TV.

"Go get me a glass of water," Mohammad would command, after I had settled in front of the TV to watch my favourite show.

"You don't have legs to walk?" I'd bark back at him. "*Ana mani khad-dameh*. I'm not your maid. Go get it yourself."

"I don't want to miss anything," he'd say, and practice his karate moves on me. When I screamed in agony, Baba would march into the room and yell, "You two are always like a rooster and chicken!" He'd switch off the TV and order us to bed.

At that time, all three of us kids slept on a mattress on the floor. The minute my dad left the room, Mohammad would start kicking me again, and my poor sister Maha wouldn't be able to get to sleep.

In 1976, عبد الله, Abdullah, was born. I was excited to have a baby brother, but I was worried that he'd be like so many other babies—always crying and making a fuss. My worries were unfounded. Abdullah was a sweet and happy baby, always smiling and laughing or sleeping like an angel. From the start, he had a very special bond with my mom. As soon as Abdullah could walk, he doted on her, telling her, "Sit, Mama," while he tried to scrub the floors for her, or grabbed a stool so that he could reach the sink to help with the dishes. Abdullah was my mom's reliable errand boy. She'd say, "حبيب قلبي, sweetheart, I need an onion and some sugar," and Abdullah would race down the street to knock on a neighbour's door, or rush after the vendors with their carts of produce. His progress was always slowed by the neighbours, saying, "Sweetheart, have a piece of bubble gum." Or, "Here's a new marble for your collec-tion." The whole neighbourhood loved Abdullah and spoiled him, but all the attention only made him sweeter and more fun-loving. Even with the typical playground conflicts or sibling rivalry, Abdullah would turn the other cheek; he never carried a grudge.

In 1979, my sister شيرين, Shireen, was born, and in 1981, هيفرون, Hivron, the baby of the family, arrived. Shireen was quiet and shy, but Hivron was born with a strong head and a stubborn attitude. She was addicted to her baby soother long after it was appropriate. Hivron had blond hair, which was highly coveted in Syria. Everyone in the neighbourhood gushed about Hivron's long blond tresses. But as any active little girl knows, long hair is a big pain in the neck. One morning, she grabbed a pair of scissors, climbed up on the sink, and cut off one of her long braids near the root.

"What have you done?" my mother screamed when she saw her. "Come here," she said to my father.

Baba just shook his head. "We have no choice but to call Uncle Mahmoud محمود," he said. Mahmoud was my mother's brother, and he had his own barbershop in Rukn al-Din. Mahmoud did his best to fix Hivron's hair, but it was cut very short.

I might have had some influence upon Hivron's act of defiance. When I was twelve or thirteen, I cut my own hair short—a sort of shag, just like Princess Diana had at her wedding.

"You look like a boy," my dad said.

I thought it looked fabulous. Since that day, my hair has never been much longer than shoulder-length.

I have shared this to show you that all during my childhood, we were a regular middle-class family, perhaps not so different from yours. Our bellies were always full, and my parents renovated the house to make room for all of us. From the window in the bedroom that Maha and I shared, we had a bird's-eye view of our neighbours' rooftops. A few neighbours kept cages of دباسي, known as laughing doves, a type of pigeon very common in Al Sham with beautiful fluffy plumage, like pink champagne. When the doves were released, they danced and swooped in the blue sky. But with a blow of the whistle, the flock would faithfully return to their rooftop home. I think of them now with fondness. I wish we could all have the certainty that no matter where we fly, home will always be there for us.

As time passed, my dad used his knowledge about medicinal plants and herbs to become an apothecary at Souq Al-Buzuriyah in central Damascus. Mama was a great seamstress with an impeccable sense of fashion, and with her big, sturdy Singer sewing machine, she made us all beautiful clothes, including more than one set of matching outfits. My parents started travelling to other countries, and they brought back stylish clothing from Turkey, Italy, and as far away as Germany.

Our house on the hill was like a hotel, with people always coming and going: relatives from Kobani, Hama, Aleppo, and Amouda, many family friends from other countries, and periodically, refugees, including Lebanese people displaced in the 1980s during the war with Israel. My father never forgot the early acts of kindness by his neighbours in Hama and Kobani when he'd been a child in need. And as soon as he had a home of his own, he had an open-door policy for anyone in need of a good meal and a place to sleep.

"But Baba," Maha and I complained when friends and family were invited into the house, "we are tired of cleaning up after people." Baba would sit us down and set us straight. "Never close your hearts or your door to people in need. Invite them into your home and give them a seat at your table."

Our friends and neighbours were from all over Syria, from Homs, Daraa, Afrin, Bosra. They were Alawite Muslims, Shia Muslims, Christians, Palestinians, Lebanese, Circassians, Westerners; we were taught to respect everyone, whatever their cultural and religious beliefs, and believe that no matter what the heritage of a person, we are all one. Everybody in our neighbourhood was like family, and we took care of each other. One of our close neighbours and my mom's best friend, Emira, was a Lebanese midwife. She attended many of the births in our neighbourhood, including Hivron's, and she always worked with a cigarette dangling from her lips. Emira adored us, especially Hivron, but she couldn't have children of her own. One day, on her way to work at the hospital, she heard the sound of a baby wailing beside a garbage bin near the entrance. It was a tiny baby girl. She took the baby inside, and when nobody came forward to claim her, Emira adopted her, naming her Samar. Samar, like Emira, her immigrant mother, fit right into our neighbourhood quilt of good people.

Goodwill was a regular way of being. If Mama and I were shopping downtown or visiting another district, and we were thirsty, we'd simply knock on a stranger's door. The resident would open the door, smile, and invite us inside for a drink. If Maha and I were returning from school on a hot June day, and we came upon a neighbour hosing off the stoop of his doorway, we would say, "Uncle, I'm thirsty," and he would hand us the hose so that we could drink that cold, fresh water, which fortified us for the remainder of our uphill walk home.

In such a multicultural place, we were always celebrating one holiday after another, from Kurdish festivals to Christian ones. Sharing a meal is very important to Syrians, so imagine how important it becomes during Ramadan, a month of fasting when you haven't eaten all day! During that month, we saw our relatives even more than usual. Each night, a different relative would host the *iftar*, the evening meal to break each day's fast. We would roll out the long plastic tablecloth, put out all the food, and then Baba would say, "الحمد لله, *Alhamdulillah*. Thank God for all this food. May God never let anyone in the world go hungry."

"Amen," we'd answer in unison.

Every morning of Ramadan started with a literal bang. Before sunrise, we would be woken up by a drum, beaten by the *mesaharati*, calling out, "Wake up for the *suhūr*," the dawn meal before the day's fast begins. All the kids loved the *mesaharati*. We would rush from our beds to the rooftop, and peer out into the darkness, to see if we could spot him coming down the road.

During Ramadan, we would also prepare for عيد الفطر, Eid al-Fitr, a three-day religious holiday that begins after Ramadan. In some ways, Eid al-Fitr is like Christmas because it involves charitable donations to people in need, money exchanges, and the sharing of lots of wonderful food with neighbours, friends, and family. It's also customary to buy new outfits for the first day of Eid, so Mama would take us to Souq Al-Hamidiyah to buy clothes and then to Souq Al-Buzuriyah to get mouth-watering spices, nuts, and homemade candies. En route, Mama would stop at the Great Mosque to say prayers, while Abdullah and I hung out in the mosque's huge courtyard, feeding the throngs of colourful laughing doves and imagining all the delicious sweets we would soon eat.

Before Eid begins, Muslims give money to people in need, a ritual called Zakat al-Fitr. Baba would give money to poor people, including our needy neighbours. On the first morning of Eid, our relatives would start to arrive, each of them giving us money. Uncle Mahmoud was always the most generous, giving us each 500 lira, which is about ten dollars—a lot of money for a child! Later in the day, we'd put on our new outfits and go to the carnivals that would spring up in every neighbourhood just for the children.

We also loved the Christian holidays. On Christmas Eve, after we had put on our pyjamas, my uncle Mahmoud would pile all us kids into his car and drive us to باب توما, the lively Christian district of Bab Tuma, to look at all the festive lights. Eventually, we'd come upon a بابا نويل, Santa Claus, or Baba Noel, standing on a corner in his red suit, and we'd call out, "Stop the car! We want to go say hi to Baba Noel!" We'd get out of the car and surround that poor street Santa. Little Hivron would fix her big eyes on his long white beard and get right up on her tiptoes to try to touch it. On the ride home, I tried hard to stay awake to drink in the lights with my thirsty eyes, but I could rarely fight off sleep.

My family began to travel more often after my parents bought their first car when I was about ten years old. We often visited Hama, my dad's birthplace, which was a three-hour drive away on the Damascus–Aleppo Highway, and every summer, we spent our vacations with relatives in Kobani. It was an idyllic place where we could roam the countryside with my uncle Khalid's sheep; feed the chickens; milk the goats; make جبنة, feta cheese, from scratch—eating it while it was still warm—and pick beautiful ripe olives from the region's orchards. I'll never forget the taste of the water from that old-fashioned well in Kobani. It was so sweet and cold, like nothing I've tasted before or since.

The popular swimming spot was نهر الفرات, the Mighty Euphrates, though the river was relatively calm as it passed through Kobani. Mohammad and Abdullah learned to swim in that river, but I never had the guts; I've always been afraid of the water. My dad would laugh and shake his head and say, "You're a Pisces, a water baby just like your brother Abdullah, but you're scared of water."

I preferred to sit on the banks of the Euphrates and watch my brothers swim, while the family enjoyed a picnic. From that spot, we could see Turkey in the distance.

"Someday, I'm going to go there to visit Istanbul," I told my brothers and sisters.

"I like it here," Abdullah would always say. He loved the country life most of all. From an early age, Kobani had a special place in his heart.

In my teen years, we holidayed in Latakia, Banivas, and Tartous, all wonderful tourist beach towns on Syria's Mediterranean. I always attempted to swim in the sea, but as soon as the water touched my knees, I felt as if I were drowning. It didn't help that Abdullah always horsed around, grabbing my leg and pulling me in.

The thing that stands out most about those years is that our house was constantly filled with people, music, and laughter. And not just because of my dad's open-door policy. My mom's kitchen was a hub for the neighbourhood women, who would pop in for فنجان قهوة, a cup of coffee, before going to the markets to shop.

Traditional Arabic *qahwah* is made by boiling the coffee grinds in water on the stovetop. Often, cardamom is added to the brew. My parents liked cardamom, and when we went to the market to buy coffee we would ask the vendor, "Could you add extra cardamom?" He would respond, "Of course, من هالعين لهالعين," an expression that means "From this eye to the other, it is a pleasure and an honour."

In my mom's kitchen, while they waited for the coffee to brew, the women would talk about their goings-on, including their dreams. That's typical in Syria and much of the Middle East: dreams have great significance and are believed to be predictive of many things—the impending weather, the political climate, and many personal issues, from potential jobs to marriages, births, and deaths. Syrians love to "read" coffee grounds, much like Westerners read their horoscopes.

Whatever the occasion, whether it was a gathering of women in my mother's kitchen, a religious holiday, or a family get-together, in our house there was always talking, singing, dancing, music, and most important, laughter. Everyone in my family had a great sense of humour, and I learned the ability to laugh, especially at myself. In general, whenever Syrians get together, we tell lots and lots of jokes, which can be difficult to translate for other cultures. But I think laughter is a universal language that can bridge any culture, and it rarely gets lost in translation when the intention is in the right place.

Friday in Muslim cultures is like Saturday in Western cultures, so the weekend would start on Thursday night, and we always had parties at my family home, which started as soon as we got home from school. The women relatives and friends would arrive with their kids and we'd play traditional Middle Eastern, Kurdish, and Bedouin music. Soon enough, the women and kids would be up on their feet, dancing. Syrian women can really let loose, mixing the traditional Arabic styles, like belly dancing and *dabke*, folk dancing (where you stand in a circle or a line, linked by your pinky fingers), with modern Western dance moves.

Abdullah was always at the centre of the party. He loved to act out roles, and he could imitate anyone in our family. He'd also pretend to be all sorts of characters, like a grumpy, hunched old shepherd who leaned on his shepherd's crook and stumbled into our dance circle. But as soon as he'd hook his pinky to the next person's, he'd suddenly transform into a young folk-dancing acrobat, doing Russian-style squats. Abdullah could make us laugh so hard that we would be doubled over, clutching our bellies and calling out, "Abdullah, stop! We can't take it anymore!"

He was also accident-prone all through his youth. When he was a boy, he stuck beans up his nose and had to be rushed to the hospital to have them dislodged. Later, when he was older and was sent on errands, he'd often move faster than his feet could carry him. Once, he fell down the steep stairs outside our house and hit his head on the concrete. He had to be rushed to the hospital for stitches. During a visit to Kobani, he backed into a kerosene lantern that shattered under his weight. That time, he needed twelve stitches. Whenever Abdullah got injured, my mom would say, "All these accidents, but he always survives. This boy is protected by *mala'ekah*," which means "protected by angels." My mother, with her gift of sight, seemed to see even then what we could not.

Chapter 2

غربة

Ghorbah

Homesick

As our family grew up, our house got bigger. My parents added another floor and a rooftop deck that gave us an even better bird's-eye view of the whole city; it was a great place to play games and socialize, and in the summer, when the house became too hot or was filled with relatives, we often slept on that rooftop under the dome of stars. In the mornings, as we hung our clothes and sheets to dry, and beat the carpets of dust, the radio station typically played the Lebanese chanteuse Fairouz. In the evenings, it was the Egyptian songstress Umm Kulthum.

The primary purpose of those two additional floors was to house Mohammad and Abdullah, and their families after they got married, which is a common practice in Syria and the Middle East; when daughters get married, they are typically expected to move into their husbands' family homes, and sons, when they marry, are usually responsible for providing the housing, often with the help of their parents.

In Muslim families, arranged marriages are still typical. A mullah will only agree to marry a woman who gives her consent. But marriages are often arranged for girls as young as fourteen. That's the age when Syrian students graduate from grade nine and write their certification exams. I did not attract the attention of suitors. The truth is that I was the ugly duckling in my family because I was the darkest among my sisters. Two of my sisters had blond hair and light skin and hazel or greenish-coloured eyes—all the coveted attributes in the Middle East. The teenage years are hard enough in any culture, but added to that for me was the humiliation of being the ugly one. I was teased mercilessly by some of my relatives, who tended to be much more traditional than my parents and other progressive Damascenes.

As a teen, I idolized Western celebrities like Madonna and Princess Diana. And much closer to home, I looked up to a glamorous flight attendant who lived in my neighbourhood. She was in her mid-twenties, single and independent. She would tell amazing stories of her global travels to exotic locales. She also brought back trendy Western gifts for me, like a pair of blue jeans.

Syria's government is a secular one, and it was very rare at that time to see women wearing a niqab to veil the face, and an abaya, a loose-fitting robe that covers the entire body. In smaller towns, some women dressed more conservatively. Many of my friends in Sham didn't have to wear the hijab at all. But after I hit puberty, some neighbours would ask Baba, "Why isn't your daughter wearing the hijab?"

"It's time for you to start wearing it," he finally told me.

I rushed to my Mama to complain. "I'm still young!" I argued. "None of my friends have to wear it. Why do I have to go out in this thing? Isn't it enough to be a good person on the inside?"

Mama was a liberal woman. "If you don't want to wear it," she said, "don't."

When I was growing up in the 1980s, many teenagers didn't go on to secondary school, which was not compulsory in Syria. A grade-nine education could get you many good jobs in Damascus. Because of that, the grade-nine exams were a national exam, and they were a big deal. Families rarely socialized during the month-long study period; all the attention was on making sure that the grade-niner in the family was studying. But with so many people coming and leaving my house, I didn't get much studying done. I'd have the book in my lap, but the words and the ideas didn't take root. I was too busy daydreaming about becoming an independent woman roaming the globe.

I failed that grade nine exam and had to repeat the year. That was tough because middle school was even stricter than grade school and I found it stifling, with its high concrete wall that made it impossible for us to see what was happening in the real world. The next year, I failed the exam again and had to repeat grade nine a third time. My parents were very disappointed, but it didn't seem important to me at the time. My mother started to worry that I would never attract a suitor. But, I reasoned, Mohammad had stopped school after grade eight to start working as a barber, and later he began travelling to Dubai and Saudi Arabia to work at salons in the Gulf region, where there appeared to be an endless supply of good money to be made, which my frugal brother was very good at saving. Why couldn't I do the same, or at least something similarly exciting? I bugged my parents a lot, and with the help of Uncle Mahmoud, I convinced them to let me get my hairdressing certificate and work at a neighbour's salon part-time.

It was a fantastic experience. I learned how to curl my hair with rollers, and I started to wear my hair in the trendy feathered hairstyle; it was worth the pain of sleeping in rollers to get those sausage curls. On my sixteenth birthday, in March, I had a big party at my house. I wore a silk blouse that changed colours in the light, a multi-coloured peasant skirt, and a thick yellow belt exactly like the one worn by Wonder Woman. In the afternoon, my six best friends came over and we put our favourite cassette tapes on the stereo, blasted music, and danced around the living room. My favourite song was "Rasputin" by Boney M. That song was released in 1978, but it took years for popular music to reach us, so it was brand new to me and my friends. We loved that it mixed disco and folky Arabic beats, and it had such a hook for a chorus. We must have played that song over and over, until our voices were hoarse from shouting out, "Rah rah rah . . ." even though we had no clue what we were shouting.

I felt so good to be sixteen and already working at a salon. Soon afterward, I started to work with my good friend Lina at her salon, which we called Sandra—Lina's favourite Western name. Our salon was actually a tiny, street-level room in her family's house. We put a chair in there and installed a mirror, but we didn't have a special salon sink, just a regular one, so when you washed a client's hair, it made a big mess.

I still have a vivid memory of one of our first guinea pigs—I mean clients. A woman came in wanting lots of light-blond highlights in her very long, dark hair. "Yes, ma'am, we can do that," we said, even though we didn't have an exact recipe for the bleaching agent. We whipped up a bleaching concoction, put a cap on her head, and set to work painting those strands. While we waited for the dye to activate, we steeped *mateh*, a drink made from yerba maté and sugar, and we whiled away the time drinking and talking with our client. The conversation must have been good, because we didn't pay much attention to her hair. When we eventually guided her to the sink and removed the cap, the bleached strands came off with the cap. We were shocked and mortified. The client looked in the mirror and asked, "Where's the blond?"

"Our bleach was probably too weak," we said. "Let's try again." On the second attempt, we put much less bleach in our concoction, kept our eyes on the timer, and her highlights came out perfect. It's a good thing she had lots of thick hair. That woman left the salon a happy customer, and as soon as she was out of range, Lina and I burst out laughing, releasing our bottled anxiety.

Even though I had found a job I loved, this did not stop my family from keeping close tabs on me, especially my busybody sister Hivron, who was the family spy. One afternoon I was at Lina's salon, the two of us engaging in our recently acquired habit of smoking cigarettes, which tasted so thrilling because we were doing it in secret. It was very hot in the salon that day and as I got up to open the front door, I saw Hivron lurking in the shadows outside, her eyes big as binocular lenses. She wagged her finger at me and said, "I caught you smoking! I'm telling Mom." And she bolted up the street.

I was tied up in knots for the rest of the afternoon, worried that if my mom heard the news, she would forbid me from working at Lina's salon. I could have killed Hivron!

When I got home, my mom called me into the kitchen. "Are you smoking?" she asked.

"Of course not," I responded, my knees shaking.

"ليش عم تكذبي, Leish 'am tikzibi, Why are you lying?" I'm not sure why I lied.

She handed me a cigarette from Baba's pack and said, "Light it."

I responded nervously. "I don't smoke!"

"You're smoking, and I don't want you to hide it from me so that I have to hear it from Hivron or the neighbours. I don't want you doing anything behind my back that you can't do in front of me."

So I came clean and confessed. From then on, I no longer hid my smoking from her.

After my sixteenth birthday, my home life changed dramatically.

My younger sister Maha had attracted the attention of a suitor. She accepted his marriage proposal and moved to Kobani, which was a two-day trip from Al Sham. Soon after, she became pregnant. She only returned home for occasional visits. I missed Maha terribly. We had shared a room and a bed for her entire life. Now that bed seemed far too big. My situation was so confusing. On the one hand, I dreamed of becoming an independent woman with a fantastic career as a hairdresser, but on the other hand, I also wanted to fall in love, get married, and have children some day. By the age of about seventeen, I had a foot in two worlds. I started working part-time in a very fancy hair salon for women, strategically located on the ground floor of an apartment building that was home to many Syrian TV and soap stars. I listened carefully to their talk of travel to exotic places. The world seemed to belong to them, and I wanted that too.

My opportunity arrived at the age of twenty. I was working at Lina's hair salon when a young woman arrived and looked me up and down ten times. "Are you the daughter of Abu Mohammad Kurdi?" she asked.

"Yes."

"I live in your neighbourhood," she said. "My sister knows an Iraqi Kurd who now lives in Canada. His name is سيروان, Sirwan. He's here for a month to find a Kurdish bride, and he wants to visit your parents."

That was code for "He wants to ask for your hand in marriage." I was very shy but also intrigued by this mystery man living halfway around the world. We set up a date for a visit with Sirwan. I was overwhelmed by excitement. "This is my dream, to move to the West," I thought.

A few days later came the knock at the door. The events that unfolded followed the traditional Muslim protocols, starting with the requirement that the prospective bride does not appear until after the suitor and other guests have settled into the living room with her parents, and that she appears only to serve Arabic coffee.

I entered the room with a silver tray of coffee and glasses of water, hoping that my shaking hands didn't betray my nerves, and trying to take in as much as possible, eyeballing Sirwan as quickly and subtly as possible before I left the room. He was much older than me. (He was in fact eleven years older.) After exiting the living room, I stood at the door trying to eavesdrop on the conversation, but it was hard to hear with my heart pounding so hard. Luckily, Hivron was working as a spy for me that afternoon, and she kept going in and out of the living room, providing me with intelligence reports. My *baba*'s interrogation of Sirwan went something like this:

"What kind of education do you have?"

"I studied law in Iraq, but I couldn't finish before we had to leave for Canada."

"How will you take care of my first daughter?"

"Right now I'm a cook at a restaurant. But I rent a nice apartment. I can provide her a good life in Canada."

To tell you the truth, I didn't really care much about the financial arrangements or whether the groom made my knees shake with love. I felt as if my dreams of living in the West were about to come true. One special provision that my father insisted upon was that we hold the marriage ceremony in Damascus and only after all the immigration paperwork was complete. That's because stories were circulating about men living in other countries coming to Syria to marry Syrian girls, only to turn around and divorce them right after the wedding and before the woman had officially gained citizenship, so that the woman was shipped back to her parents like a box of shattered dishes. My father was determined to protect me from such a fate.

Once Sirwan left, my mom sat down beside me, grabbed my hand, and said, "He seems like a good guy. What do you think about going to Canada?"

"I have butterflies, but I want to go," I said.

"It's so far away," Mom replied, but she smiled and squeezed my hand to hide her sorrow.

My dad came into the room. "You're a piece of my heart; you're special to me," he said. "I don't know what your future will be. This guy might turn out to be a good guy or a bad guy. But it's your decision."

That was the start of a whirlwind of exciting times in my life. A few days later, Sirwan came to take me to the Jewish district to buy gold. A week later, we had the engagement party. I wore a pink princess gown covered in sparkling beads and I made sure my hair looked effortlessly feathered. Soon after that, I began the first stage of the bureaucratic process to get my visa. I got to know the Canadian embassy office very well. All the people there were so nice and friendly, saying, "Vancouver is a very beautiful place."

After I got my Canadian visa, Sirwan returned for the wedding, which we had on our family's rooftop deck. I designed my gown to look like a flower blossom, but it didn't turn out the way I had imagined. I think I looked more like a marshmallow. We honeymooned at the Sheraton for two nights, and then all my family and friends said their final goodbyes at a party at my home, the night before I departed for Canada.

The flight to Canada was my first airplane trip. I dressed up for the occasion. I wore an elegant white suit, with a fitted skirt and a jacket with a peplum ruffle at the waist. I felt so stylish and grown-up. My whole family came to the airport to see us off. That's when it hit me that I was really leaving my family, with no clue when I'd see them again.

"I'm going to miss you so much," I cried to my brothers and sisters, and especially Mama and Baba, whom I must have kissed and hugged a hundred times before my boarding call was announced.

"Call me as soon as you're safe in your new home," said Mama, her face wet with tears.

"Come back to visit us as soon as you can and as often as you can," said Baba, trying not to cry.

On the plane, my tears kept flowing for many hours. They certainly didn't match the sophistication of that white suit. Before we landed, I went to the washroom to freshen up my makeup, and—I'm blushing with the memory of what I did next—I put my wedding tiara on my head. When I emerged from the airplane washroom in my tiara, the passengers started to clap. I felt exhilarated, like a princess walking down an aisle strewn with roses.

When we landed in Canada, crowds of Sirwan's friends were waiting to greet us. They had dressed up in traditional Kurdish clothes to make me feel welcome. But many of Sirwan's friends didn't speak Arabic; they only spoke Iraqi Kurdish, which is different from the Syrian Kurdish dialect, so I couldn't communicate with them very well.

My new husband had rented a beautiful apartment for us in North Vancouver, a mountainside suburb across the harbour from downtown Vancouver. It was like a mirage to me, gleaming and sparkling with high-rises, surrounded by water and green mountains. Unlike in Syria, my new home was at the bottom rather than at the top of a mountain, in a ground-floor apartment with a little patio that had a peekaboo view of the Lions Gate Bridge. When I woke up on my first morning in Canada, I jumped out of bed, so excited to explore my new world. I called my parents to tell them that I'd arrived safely. As soon as I heard my mother's voice, I started to cry.

"Please tell me you'll come home every year to visit," she said.

Through my tears, I promised her. "I will be back every year. Nothing will stop me," I said. I also told her that I couldn't wait to become a mother.

I spent a great deal of time on the edge of downtown at the home of one of Sirwan's Kurdish friends. She was friendly and welcoming, but she didn't speak much Arabic. She and her husband had six kids, ranging in age from two to thirteen. They quickly became my surrogate family. I went there virtually every day, and sometimes I slept there at night too, because my husband worked long shifts at the restaurant, and after work he would often socialize with his Kurdish friends. I began to learn English at the same time that my son, Alan, did. We would spend time with her kids, watching *Barney* and playing dolls with them, and I would study their elementary and junior high school homework. But I found it a difficult language to learn, and I could barely communicate with anyone.

My first days and years in Vancouver were very tough. I ached for my family: the early morning coffees with my mom, my dad with his herbal concoctions and his sage words, the big, delicious family meals, the weekly dance parties with my aunties and sisters and cousins, Abdullah's jokes and stories that made us quake with laughter. Instead, I had to settle for brief, rushed weekly phone calls. I became terribly homesick. The common Arabic word for that feeling of estrangement—of being torn from your roots, of having a big hole in your heart that can never be filled or patched—is *ghorbah*.

Soon after my arrival, I became pregnant, which made for even more *ghorbah*, especially for my mom. The first few months of my pregnancy, I was so nauseated that I barely ate, and I lost weight when I should have been gaining it. Then I discovered McDonald's french fries; strangely, they were the only thing I could keep down. I guess I ate too much McDonald's because in the last three months of my pregnancy, I got fat. I didn't get much exercise—no more daily climbs up steep hills and stairways. And when the autumn came, it rained a lot, so I spent much of my time indoors. The damp of Vancouver soon got into my bones, and the clouds and endless grey unsettled my mind too.

Springtime was a welcome reprieve. The stately maples and oaks donned bright-green leaves, and the rhododendrons and tulips woke up after their long sleeps, exploding with colours. In my bright yellow raincoat, I was so pregnant I looked like I was about to explode too.

My son, Alan, was born in April 1993. We named him Alan after the Alana Valley, the region where my husband had grown up in Kurdistan. I loved being a mother, but the experience made me feel even more *ghorbah*, for my family. I longed again for my mother. I felt even closer to her now that I had my own baby. My happiest memory of that time is my first trip back to Damascus in the summer of 1994, so that my family could meet my son, Alan.

Chapter 3

يا عمري انتي

Ya omri enti

You Are My Life

The minute the plane crossed the spine of mountains and the lights of my home city appeared below, my heart began to pound with excitement.

"I cannot wait for the plane to land so that you can meet your family," I said to Alan.

As soon as the airplane doors opened, I took huge gulps of the jasmine-scented air, and when I hit the tarmac, I wanted to kiss the ground. I reached the customs guard and I beamed from ear to ear when he said, "*Ahla w sahla fi baladek,* Warm welcome to your country." I could hardly bear waiting for my luggage, knowing my family was now so close. When I finally saw them, I burst into tears of joy and rushed into their arms.

Alan's eyes were huge saucers as more than a dozen relatives hugged and kissed him. We piled into the packed car, and Abdullah, now eighteen years old, took Alan on his lap and started chattering away to him in pidgin English. His conversation made no sense to anyone but baby Alan, who replied in his own chirpy baby talk.

"Alan is teaching me English," Abdullah said in Arabic. They were fast friends.

When the car got into Al Sham, I stuck my head out the window and breathed deeply, filling my head with the dreamy air of my city: of jasmine and rose, of roasted spices, of sun-warmed mountains and the sweet, cool flavor of the Baruda River that quenched the entire city. Once home, I was hit by that other unique smell—that of the family home, as unique as a fingerprint. It smelled like love, like belonging. I opened every door and went into every room, drinking in the pictures and photos on the wall, the furniture, and most of all, the view of the neighbourhood and the city, every window framing a living picture. The whole time, my family watched me and laughed. Alan had just started walking, so Abdullah took him by the hand and guided us into the kitchen, saying, "*Teta*, your grandmother, made your mama's favourite dish. Smell the *waraq inab*, stuffed grape leaves." We took Alan to the rooftop and admired the view.

"There's nothing in the world like this," I said. I felt I was floating on the silky air.

Abdullah was exactly the same, a lighthearted practical joker. On that first homecoming, I brought him a whoopee cushion.

"Let's play a joke on Baba," he whispered to Alan. At the first opportunity, Abdullah placed it under Baba's seat cushion. When it erupted, Baba jumped up in shock. The look on his face made us burst out laughing.

After six glorious weeks at home, I said goodbye to my family again and Alan and I went back to our lives in Vancouver, which were, by comparison, much more somber. My marriage became increasingly strained, and it was an even greater solace to return to Al Sham each summer. In 1996, I separated from my husband. It was my choice. He was a wonderful father to Alan, and he tried very hard to be a good husband, but our relationship wasn't working. When I called home and told my father I was getting a divorce, he was so upset.

"Come back to Damascus immediately," he demanded.

"That is impossible," I responded. "Alan's father won't like the idea of me taking Alan so far away, and I'm not going to abandon my son."

My father didn't want that either, and in hindsight I recognize that he was worried about how I'd survive as a single mother. But at the time, I interpreted his orders as cruel ultimatums. The divorce put a rift between me and my family, one that lasted five long years. The estrangement from my family made life as a new immigrant even more difficult. I talked to my mom every so often, but the conversations were rushed and awkward.

By that time I was living in East Vancouver in a shabby rental apartment building that was home to many single mothers and their children. I could still barely speak English, but I needed to find work. Some of my ex-husband's Kurdish friends were delivering local newspapers. They suggested I apply, and I was offered a job working the overnight shift on the newspaper's printing press, putting advertising inserts into the newspapers. While I worked, I was able to leave Alan sleeping with my friend Iris, a Chinese immigrant with a child of her own, or with Sirwan. At first, that job made me feel even more like a foreigner in a strange land. I was lonely, miserable, and exhausted. Working the assembly line, you had to be alert and work fast. I barely opened my mouth to my co-workers, many of whom were also immigrants, from the Philippines, India, and Pakistan. They had as much trouble speaking English as I did.

I couldn't wait for those nights to end so that I could rush back home to Alan. I loved being a mother, and every hour apart from my boy filled me with pain, anxiety, and guilt.

One night while I was at work, the stress and exhaustion were overwhelming. I started to cry, and the tears plopped onto the newspaper ink. Linda, the night shift supervisor, noticed me and came over. I thought I was going to be fired, but she said nothing. Instead, she just worked alongside me. The next night, she did the same thing, but this time she taught me a new English word and said she would keep doing this—a new word every night.

I worked at that job for about two years. Linda gradually became a great friend and ally. She sometimes came to my home, bringing toys for Alan and taking us sightseeing. On one of her visits, I told her that I used to be a hairdresser back in Sham.

"I need a good haircut. Can you do it?" she asked. I took her into my tiny bathroom and gave her a haircut.

"Wow," she said, looking at herself in the mirror. "Are you certified?"

"I went to school in Damascus and I worked in a salon there, but I haven't had any official training in Canada."

Linda helped me apply to a local hairdresser school so that I could get my certification. After a couple of months of introductory lessons, one of the teachers approached me as I was leaving class.

"You're wasting your time and money here," she told me. "I know an Italian guy with a salon who needs a hairdresser. You should work with him."

"But I'm still not certified," I said.

"With your skills and experience, that shouldn't be a problem. Call him," she said, handing me a phone number.

It was 1998, and I got the job with her friend at a high-end hair salon on Robson Street in Vancouver. The clientele were great and so were the tips. New clients would often ask, "Where are you from?" When I told them, few knew where Syria was. Only when I said "Next to Lebanon" could they picture my country on a map. Many people had problems pronouncing my name—Fatima. When my boss was ordering my new business cards, he said, "Why don't you call yourself Tima?" I liked it, and ever since then, most English-speaking people have called me Tima. Even my brothers and sisters started calling me Tima sometimes too.

The staff at the salon were a close-knit bunch; they embraced me and my son, and we soon became dear friends. I became the independent Western woman that I had spent my childhood daydreaming about. I had a great group of girlfriends, and we sometimes went out to restaurants and cafes on a Friday night. I met some men who wanted to date. But I wasn't interested. My only priority was my son, and I would not settle ever again for anyone whom I wasn't in love with, nor for any man who could not make a serious, loving commitment to my son.

After a few years of saving my good wages from the salon, I could finally afford to return to Damascus. It was 2002, and Alan was now nine years old. That homecoming is burned into my memory. My family had grown so much since I had left, and there were many new faces in the crowd. Mohammad had married Ghouson, a beautiful, tall, willowy woman who had also grown up in Rukn al-Din. They now lived on the third floor of our family house and had two young kids, a daughter named Heveen and a baby boy named Shergo. Maha made the trek from Kobani for our reunion, with her brood of six kids: her fourteen-year-old daughter Rodeen, followed by Adnan, Barehan, Fatima (named after me), Mahmoud, and Yasmeen. I didn't even recognize my sister Shireen. Shireen was twenty-three. She had married a carpenter named Lowee, and they lived in our neighbourhood, in a house strategically located about halfway between our home on the mountaintop and the bottom of that steep street—the perfect place to make a pitstop and have a tea

33

when you were returning from the markets laden with groceries. Shireen and Lowee had two small boys, Yasser and Farzat.

And my little spy Hivron. She was twenty and all grown up now. She had caught the eye of a boy named Ahmad, who lived a stone's throw from our house. He was not an ideal suitor in our uncle Mahmoud's opinion. "He's so young; he has nothing. You're young and beautiful. You could have any husband you like," he told her. But Hivron fought hard for Ahmad.

"I'm in love! It's him or nobody."

She was very determined, and as I said before, when Hivron is determined, she gets her way. Hivron had three young kids, two daughters named Rawan and Ghoufran, and a son named Abdulrahman.

Then there was Abdullah, who wasn't a clumsy, happy-go-lucky young boy anymore. He was twenty-six years old—all grown up with a five o'clock shadow on his chiselled face. Still, his sweet, fun-loving character and his smile were just as huge and contagious as ever. He had travelled a bit to other countries in the Middle East, but he preferred Syria and now worked at Mohammad's salon. Abdullah had yet to fall in love, and he still lived with my parents on the second floor of our house.

The biggest shock of all was seeing my mother. My beautiful, vivacious mother had aged and seemed much older than her fifty-one years. Her health had deteriorated dramatically over the years: her diabetes had become quite debilitating and she had heart problems, which ran in her family. At the Sham airport, I knelt down and kissed her swollen feet, crying, "Forgive me for being away for so long."

To which my dear mother replied, in her usual way, "You are a piece of my heart. *Ya omri enti*," meaning, "You are my life."

We returned to the house, which smelled as it always did—like home. My mom's illness was written on her face and body, but that didn't stop her from cooking up my favourite foods: beef dolma, *mahshi* (stuffed zucchini and eggplant), and especially kibbeh, a dough made with bulgur wheat and stuffed with mouth-watering ingredients. I ate a lot on that trip, but I burned off much of it, getting reacquainted with my city and, of course, dancing it off during our nightly parties. I captured many hours of that trip to Sham with a video camera. The footage shows us strolling around the streets of Damascus, relaxing during coffee breaks at local cafes, and dancing—so much dancing. Mohammad's wife, Ghouson, is a supple reed, drinking up the camera's spotlight. Hivron shows off a pair of white silk pyjamas that my friend Iris gave me in Vancouver. Maha's daughter Fatima hasn't even hit puberty, and Alan is still a boy, but he towers over his cousins Heveen and Abdulrahman; Yasser and Shergo are chubby toddlers with big fat pink cheeks. The only difference then compared to when we were young is that several of us danced with our own kids propped on our hips.

It was a wonderful trip, but my mother's deteriorating health cast a shadow upon those weeks. Just before I left, we had a very solemn conversation. She held my hand and said, "Promise me that you'll take care of Abdullah and help him find a good wife."

I didn't want to hear that. "You will be the one to find Abdullah a wife," I said. Her face became drawn.

When I kissed her goodbye at the airport and said, "I'll see you next year," the same stricken look invaded her face. That was the last time I saw her.

Soon after that trip, my mom got very sick and became bedridden. Eventually she was hospitalized, and for many months she was in and out of the hospital. All my siblings visited her daily, but Abdullah remained the most devoted to her and was at her bedside constantly. I felt every millimetre of our ten-thousand-kilometre separation. My family had a home phone by then, so I talked to them daily, using long-distance calling cards so that I could reach them from home or from work. One morning, before work, I couldn't reach my family, so I called Uncle Mahmoud on his cellphone.

"I can't talk right now. I'll call you later," he said, and hung up. His tone revealed nothing, but I had a sinking feeling that something terrible had happened to my mom. I had the urge to burst into tears. But I needed to keep it together and get to work. I was short-tempered with Alan as I rushed to get him ready for school.

I had back-to-back appointments at work and I could not afford to take even a ten-minute break until that afternoon. I went to the private area at the back of the salon and the waterworks began. When my boss and my co-worker asked what was wrong, I confessed. "Something is wrong with Mama. I just can't work." They were understanding and let me call my uncle Mahmoud again.

"Uncle, be honest, what's wrong with my mother?" I cried.

"We are all in God's hands," he responded.

"What do you mean? Is my mom dead?"

"*Allah yerhamha*," he responded, meaning, "May God rest her soul in peace."

I sunk to the floor and started to bawl. "Don't bury her yet," I begged. "I want to come. I want to hold her hand and kiss her cheek one last time. I want to say goodbye."

"That's not possible, Fatima," Mahmoud said gently. "Come at the one-year anniversary."

I immediately left work and went straight home. Once I arrived, I called my family in Sham. Baba answered. I could hear the Koran being recited in the background. I don't remember if we said anything. I think we just cried. Eventually, my *baba* passed the phone to Abdullah.

"How am I going to continue my life? I feel so lost," said Abdullah. I was trying to comfort him when the phone card ran out of money and the connection between us broke.

We have an expression in Syria that Allah will put a wall between the deceased and the living, which grows thicker over time, so that the family can move on with their lives. But this is easier to say than to do. After Mama died, Abdullah sunk into a depression. For my father's sake, he tried to put a good face on it, and my other siblings did their best to spend time with my *baba*. Mohammad's family was right upstairs, and Hivron and Shireen brought their families to the house every Friday to spend the day with him. But my siblings had busy lives of their own. It must have been a very lonely and difficult time for Abdullah and my father, two solitary men rattling around in that house, trying to remain brave around each other but privately mourning their favourite lady.

The summer after my mom's death, I returned to Sham to visit her grave and honour her life. Even with the house filled with family for my visit, it was empty without her, a huge hole in the middle of our lives. My dad had a large photograph of her framed and placed on the wall, so that he and Abdullah could eat every single meal with her. "Try the kibbeh," Abdullah would say to her. "It's not as good as yours."

In Islamic cultures, when a loved one dies, the mourners are expected to perform an act of charity to someone in need, on behalf of the deceased. When I returned to Sham, I ordered a hundred chickens from the local butcher. The next day, I sent the kids to knock on doors. When the inhabitants answered the door, the kids said, "Our auntie sent us to give you this chicken on behalf of my grandmother's soul." The recipients would humbly accept the offering, and respond, "*Allah yerhamha*, May your grandmother's soul rest in peace."

I also visited our family's olive grove in Kobani, which my dad and my brothers had planted on our land a few years before my mom died. Baba said, "Olive trees can live and thrive for hundreds of years, and they're hardy and drought-resistant. If we grow olives, everyone can live off the proceeds for a year." Of course, it takes at least five years for olive trees to grow up and bear fruit, but my father is a very patient man when he wants to be.

Throughout the first decade of the twenty-first century, I returned home at least every second summer. Damascus grew a little bit more on every visit, but from my rooftop perch at the top of the mountain, time seemed to stand still. The call to prayer greeted me each morning, and each day, after getting my Arabic *qahwah*—coffee—I ran to the window to hear the calls of the vendors as the city shook off its sleep. During my summer visits in 2005, I woke up every day to the sound of my cellphone ringing. On the line was a man named Rocco, an Italian-Canadian I had met the previous year. Over the past few months, we had gotten to know each other. My co-workers had weekly volleyball games at Kits Beach every Sunday, and Rocco had begun to show up for those games. Like me, he wasn't much of a volleyball player, but Rocco and my son, Alan, bonded right away. Alan was only twelve years old, but he was wise beyond his years, and he had a knack for assessing people's characters. It was a good sign that he liked Rocco. When Rocco asked me out on a date before I was about to go back to Sham, it was tempting. But my family had been pressuring me to find a nice Syrian man; my sisters had a few suitors in mind that they wanted me to meet. I told Rocco that I might no longer be single by the time I returned from Sham, but he didn't give up.

"Can I call you while you're there?" he asked. I said he could. Rocco worked in sales, and with those daily phone calls to me in Sham, it became clear that he was an expert at his trade.

We were married in 2006, in Rocco's home city of Toronto. It was a big Italian wedding, and my family was unable to travel all the way to Canada for it. Alan walked me down the aisle, and my dear friend Iris was my maid of honour; I even hired a belly dancer to bring a touch of Al Sham to the party. I missed my family terribly, but I got something of a taste of home when we honeymooned in Montreal. It was the first place in North America that reminded me of Sham—the old buildings and narrow medieval-looking alleyways, the active, outdoor social lifestyle, the cafes and bars and wonderful restaurants that served so much delicious Middle Eastern cuisine.

Back in Vancouver, we moved into a nice backsplit-style house in Coquitlam, with a backyard deck off the kitchen and a yard that was large enough for me to have a vegetable patch to grow cucumbers and juicy, organic tomatoes. I added another touch of the Sham life to the yard, growing grapes on a big cedar trellis so that I could sit in the sun-dappled shade, drinking coffee and socializing with friends.

Rocco and I wanted to have more children, and we even did IVF treatments, which ultimately failed. It was devastating not to be able to have more children, but I had to accept it.

Rocco's job in sales involved travelling extensively, first in Canada and later in the Far East. In 2011, I left my job at the salon so that Rocco and I could move to Shanghai, where we lived until 2013. During that time, I had a flexible schedule and the freedom to travel with Rocco to exotic places around the globe, including the Philippines, Hong Kong, Singapore, and Bangkok.

Before I moved to Shanghai, I visited Syria every summer, or every second summer, sometimes with Alan and Rocco, and a few times on my own. I would spend four to six weeks at a time back in Syria. In between visits, I talked to my family at least once a week on the phone; later, when Internet and video calling became available, my uncle Mahmoud was the first to start using it, so my family would call me when they went to his house to visit.

Each year that I returned to Sham, I found myself in a city that was a little more Western, a little more modern. Amusement parks and Internet cafes opened up, sushi restaurants became popular, and many people started carrying around cellphones. Yet I could still go back to the Ancient City and get lost in its labyrinth of wonderful treasures; the places I loved most in Sham hadn't changed. And the jasmine still grew wild everywhere, cascading from balconies and courtyards, spilling out of pots, pouring over the ancient stone walls, and sprouting through the cobblestones.

For my family members—most of them self-employed with small businesses—it was a time of stability, growth, and increased prosperity, much as it had been for my mom and dad's generation. Mohammad's salon was doing well, and he and Ghouson had two more children. Shireen now had three boys in total. Maha was still living in Kobani, and she had a whopping eight kids. Hivron had five kids, and she was still living with her in-laws, but they had also built a summer house of their own, near Yarmouk, a suburb of Sham. My teenaged nieces and nephews in Sham had summertime jobs that earned them enough money to buy cellphones and running shoes.

Abdullah was still living with my *baba* in Sham. Abdullah was thirty-three years old, and he didn't have his eyes on anyone. Whenever one of us suggested a woman to him, she wasn't his cup of tea; he didn't much care for any of the women that we suggested. He wanted to make the decision for himself. He didn't want to be rushed and prodded by his loving but very bossy sisters into making the choice.

Late in the summer of 2010, just after I had returned to Canada from one of my summer visits, Abdullah went to Kobani with my dad and Mohammad to tend to our family's olive orchard, which had begun to produce nice, ripe olives—not too many, but it was a start, and those first few harvests made our family a little money. Abdullah was working at the orchard when he saw a dark-haired young woman. Her name was ريحانة. In Arabic, *Rehan* is the name of the aromatic herb basil, and her family called her that. But other Arabic people called her Rehanna. She was twenty-two and very shy, but Abdullah soon discovered that she was our second cousin. In Syria, it's quite common to marry second cousins, and Abdullah fell hard for Rehanna.

That September, I got a call from Abdullah saying, "Rehanna and I are going to buy our rings today."

I cried with joy. "*Mabrouk!* Congratulations! Mama will be very happy," I said. I looked up to the sky and said to my mama in heaven, "I honoured your wish."

I couldn't make it back to Syria for Abdullah's engagement party, but I called him during the celebration. I had to yell to be heard over the Kurdish and Bedouin music blasting in the background; it sounded like the whole town of Kobani was there to celebrate.

One month later, the happy couple returned to Sham, where my family hosted a small, casual wedding at our home. My siblings sent me an endless stream of photos of Abdullah and his beautiful bride. When I saw the way they looked at each other, I knew that Abdullah had found his soulmate.

A month later, Abdullah called me.

"Rehanna is pregnant. But nine months is too long to wait," he said. "I'm so happy. I can't believe I'm going to be a father!"

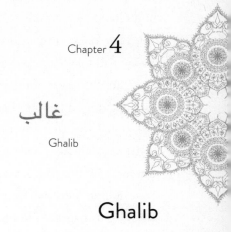

Chapter 4

غالب

Ghalib

Ghalib

I got to meet Rehanna for the first time on my next visit to Damascus, the following April of 2011. I loved her immediately. She was a bit shy with me at first, but she was always smiling, and, like Abdullah, she had a great sense of humour, and he loved to make her laugh. At that time, Rehanna was seven months pregnant. I was so excited for them that I brought them all the necessities for their baby—clothes, shoes, blankets, bibs, rattles, soothers. I had bought so many things for that baby that I needed to pack an extra suitcase. I was there with Abdullah and Rehanna for her ultrasound, which revealed that they were having a boy. Abdullah was over the moon. When we got back home, we rushed to Baba, and Abdullah told him the good news, saying, "ألف مبروك, *Alf mabrouk.*

Congratulations! You're going to have a grandson, and I'm going to name him Ghalib after you."

That night, the whole family came to our house to celebrate. As always, Abdullah cracked us up the entire time.

"Stop it! You're going to bring the baby early," cried Rehanna.

The only difference between those family parties and the parties of our youth was that my nieces and nephews were now doing hip-hop and breakdancing, having learned the steps from satellite TV and the Internet. Life on the streets of Damascus seemed just as it always had, even though there had been protests against the government. In Daraa, a group of teenagers were imprisoned for spray-painting anti-regime messages. There were reports that some police officers and protesters had been killed. By the time I arrived in Sham in April, the protests had spread to Latakia, Homs, and Hama. Initial calls for democracy and freedom were soon replaced by calls to overthrow the government.

On TV, we watched coverage of these protests.

"What do the people want?" I asked my dad.

"بدّن الحرية, *Baddon al-hurriya.* They say they want freedom, but I'm not sure what they mean by that."

As with so much else during those early days, and ever since, it was hard to know who to believe. Information from the many news sources varied so much, it was like reading the coffee grounds: the analysis depended on the viewpoint. Some protesters wanted economic reform. Others wanted political reform and democratic elections. Maybe another factor was the growing number of university-educated young adults who craved the freedoms of the West, and all this fervor was stoked by the Arab Spring that had swept Tunisia and Egypt in early 2011.

We were shocked when the protests erupted into greater violence so quickly, and they spread like a sandstorm. Had citizens suddenly turned

against each other? Or was this the fault of a small number of extrem-
ists on both sides of the growing divide? Foreign instigators? And what
part did international powers play in these early days and months of the
uprising? When my family discussed the political climate, the consensus
was that nobody wanted our peaceful country to dissolve into sectarian
violence. We all worried that such violence would turn back the clock of
progress.

Before I left for Sham, Rocco had registered me with the Canadian
embassy. I thought he was just being unduly cautious, so it was a surprise
when the embassy called in the midst of my trip and advised me to leave.
With the streets of Sham so peaceful, it was hard to take their warning
seriously.

It was a challenge to read the pulse of Syrians during those early
days of the uprising, and ever since, in part because Syrians are intensely
private people. I grew up in a culture that had always opened its doors to
people of all stripes and shades, surrounded by people who had always
gone out of their way to make others feel welcome. I'm not a political
person, or at least I wasn't at that time. I was like most those around the
world. As long as my family and my close friends and colleagues were
happy, healthy, and safe, I was happy too. And no matter the specific
traditions of religion or sect, my impression was, and still is, that Syrians
have always bonded over the things that stitch together the fabric of daily
life—love, marriage, births, deaths, jobs, weather, cultural trends, food,
drink, music, dance, sorrow, and laughter.

Abdullah and Rehanna were thinking only of their future son.
Rehanna's clothes were tight, so I said, "Let's go shopping for some new
clothes at Souq Al-Hamidiyah," the beating heart of the Old City. We
went with my sisters to the market, where we strolled beneath its huge
iron vault, like a long rib cage, filled with shops. Rehanna bought a few

lightweight summer dresses, and then we strolled through the *souq*, which flows into Umayyad Mosque, where we sat in the giant mosaic-tiled courtyard among the laughing doves.

"I'm going to go in and pray for an easy birth," Rehanna said.

"Pray for us too," Abdullah said.

When Rehanna came out, she was hungry. "You can't be hungry, we just ate," said Abdullah. "It must be my boy who needs the food."

"Let's go to Beit Jeddi, My Grandfather's House," I said. It was a famous restaurant.

We got to that beautiful old converted mansion, and Rehanna started to laugh, her swollen belly shaking; she always covered her mouth when she laughed.

"I thought you were taking me to *your* grandfather's house," she said.

We sat at a table in the courtyard, beneath the dangling curtains of rose and jasmine blossoms, eating our fill of *mashawi* (mixed grilled meats) and *foul mudammas*, a spicy fava bean dish. I ordered too much food and Abdullah said, "We're all eating for two, tonight."

The evening had been so peaceful that I was surprised when someone from the Canadian embassy called me again. It was only ten days before I was scheduled to fly back to Vancouver.

"We're instructing Canadian citizens to leave," the woman from the embassy said.

"Are the embassy and the airport closing?" I asked.

"No."

"Then I'm staying."

I received a final shock when my uncle Waleed drove me to the airport in the early hours of May 14, 2011. We were confronted en route by a number of military checkpoints, and at each one we had to present our ID.

"What's going on?" Uncle Waleed asked each officer.

"Just a routine check" was the response.

"إن شاء الله, *Inshallah*, the situation will calm down soon enough, Fatima," my uncle said.

We believed everything would be fine.

In July 2011, just a few weeks before Rehanna's due date, she and Abdullah left Sham for Kobani. The decision was only partly based on "the situation" in Syria. Rehanna was a small-town girl at heart, and she was the eldest of eight kids; she was very close with her father, who relied on her to help with all the family decision-making. And like so many people, she wanted to share her newborn son with her big family. It was an added bonus that Kobani remained so peaceful, as many other parts of the country grew increasingly unstable.

As her due date drew closer, Rehanna was told she'd need a C-section. Abdullah wanted Rehanna to have the best possible care, so they travelled to Manbij (an hour's drive southwest of Kobani) with my sister Maha and Rehanna's parents. I sent the money to pay for the operation. The delivery was complicated, but everything turned out fine, and on July 8, Abdullah and Rehanna's eldest son, غالب, Ghalib, was born.

I called my brother the following morning.

"*Alhamdulillah*. Thank God, Rehanna and the baby are in good health. This baby is so small. *Ana sirt ab*. I'm a father now. Maha says he looks like me."

I was startled by my little brother's tone. It was so deep and resonant but so calm at the same time, carrying all the many privileges and responsibilities of fatherhood.

"ألف مبروك, a thousand congratulations," I said. "I'll call Baba with the good news."

47

"Tell him we have a baby Ghaliboo," said Abdullah, referring to his nickname for our dad.

Baba was so happy. "*Alhamdulillah!* I can't wait to meet the new Ghalib in the family. Abdullah has such a good heart to name his son after me. I know he's going to be a great father. That boy is the only thing he has talked about for nine months."

It was another revelation when, a few days later, after the family was back home in Kobani, I heard Abdullah speaking to his son, saying, "*Habibi*, talk to your عمة *Ammeh*, Auntie Fatima." His voice had that beautiful new pitch that a loving father reserves for his baby. And as for me, I'd experienced the privilege of becoming an aunt many times already. But now I felt something extra, as if I had honoured my pledge to my mom to help Abdullah have a family.

In his first two years of life, Ghalib was a crybaby, just like I was as a child. Nobody knew what was wrong with him, but whatever his early-life ailments, they disappeared when he learned to walk. Rehanna and my sister Maha grew very close during those years. Rehanna and Ghalib came to visit Maha every day at noon so that they could prepare the big daily meal together. As soon as Ghalib could talk, he called Maha *Teta*, Grandma, even though my sister was very young, with rosy cheeks, and not the boy's grandmother. In the evenings, Rehanna, Abdullah, and baby Ghalib often returned to Maha's rooftop patio to drink tea and watch the world go by.

Rehanna's dad and brothers built a simple, concrete one-bedroom house for Rehanna and Abdullah. It was still attached to her family's home, but it gave Abdullah's young family some privacy. Abdullah also set up a salon at the front of their house, but it was hard to get clients in Kobani. The lack of work worried Abdullah, but Maha told me that Rehanna always had a way of calming Abdullah.

"*Inshallah*, you could touch the sand and turn it into gold. It will get so much better in the future," she would always say.

Rehanna loved to do embroidery, and she had a sewing machine that could make special patterns on cloth. She was so good at embroidery that her friends and neighbours would hire her to make beautiful, personalized patterns on blankets, pillowcases, and duvet covers.

"Rehanna was so easygoing," Maha recalled. "She always said, 'We have tomatoes, hot chilies, and bread. What more do we need?'" In many ways, Rehanna was just like my *baba*. She felt rich if she was with family and they had the basic provisions of life.

Despite Rehanna's positive attitude, though, Abdullah couldn't turn sand into money to pay the bills. Soon after Ghalib's birth, they started commuting to Damascus, where they would stay during the week so that Abdullah could find enough clients to make money. It wasn't an easy decision, as travelling across Syria had become increasingly risky.

On the eve of Ramadan in July 2011, hundreds of people in Hama, my father's birthplace, were killed when they were caught in the middle of the fight between the regime and the rebels. Many citizens had no choice but to flee to the big cities of Damascus and Aleppo to seek work and safety. Soon there were rebel groups everywhere, and fighting had spread from Idlib province in the northwest, to my summer vacation region of Latakia on the Mediterranean, to the suburbs of Damascus. By October, people began to utter the words that almost no one in Syria wanted to hear: civil war.

The rebels went on the loudspeaker at the local mosque in Rukn al-Din, calling out for all men between the ages of eighteen and forty to join the rebel groups. Like so many other civilians, no one in my family wanted to take one side or the other.

"It's crazy here now," said Abdullah over the phone. "Both sides expect us to take up a rifle and point it at our friends and neighbours. I'm not risking my life and my family's lives. You don't even know who or what you're fighting for or against. *Inshallah*, life will return to its old peacefulness, but that seems more like a dream every day."

In our neighbourhood of Rukn al-Din, rebel groups set up head-quarters in the streets, while the government had taken over the top of Mount Qasioun. My family and others were literally caught in the cross-fire of intermittent battles.

One morning, after a near-sleepless night with gunfire constantly crackling in the distance, Rehanna and baby Ghalib went over to Hivron's for a visit. "I'm putting all my kids down," said Hivron, after Rehanna had put baby Ghalib down. Hivron made some tea, and the two women tried to enjoy some quiet adult conversation. Suddenly they heard the crack and whistle of a missile so loud that it woke up all the kids.

"يا الله، أختي, Oh my God, sister. Is it coming in our direction?" asked Hivron, running to the window. Ghalib started to wail and the other kids came running or hid under blankets. Everyone listened to the whistle, waiting for its horrifying pitch to end in an explosion—how close, no-body knew. Five seconds, ten. Then, finally, there was an explosion in the distance.

Hivron lost it. She opened the window and screamed, "Stop it, you animals! Don't you care about the kids? We're tired of this bloody war. What are you fighting for?" She yelled into the void until her husband, Ahmad, came out, saying, "Shh. Are you crazy? Close the window."

After that incident, Abdullah packed up their remaining possessions and took Rehanna and Ghalib back to Kobani. From then on, Abdullah would come on his own and stay with Baba whenever he was in Sham for work.

"You wouldn't recognize our neighbourhood, our city," Abdullah la-mented in one of our daily phone calls. "Armed men that I've never seen before come right up to me and demand to know, 'Who are you? Where do you come from? Who do you support? Bashar or the rebels?' You don't know which team they're on. You can't say, 'Where did *you* come from?' We just show our ID and answer their questions. It's too dangerous here now for Rehanna and Ghalib. Thank God it's still safe in Kobani."

"It's a nightmare," Hivron told me when I called her soon after. "We don't know what's going to happen from one minute to the next. You go out to the market, and when you come back, you see strange men standing on your street corner with machine guns, asking, 'Who are you?' I ask them, 'Who are *you*?' Sometimes they don't even answer. They just look at you like you're a stone."

In 2012, the conflict went from bad to worse. Mohammad's son Shergo, who was twelve at that time, happened upon a protest and saw a school friend drop dead from a bullet to the neck. The boy was shot by a police officer. Shergo ran to Mohammad and Abdullah's salon, and they locked the shutters until it was safe enough to return home. Increasingly, clashes between rebels and military erupted in Rukn al-Din near the salon. There was no safety at any hour of the day. In our neighbourhood and many other districts, bands of armed gangs began to raid houses and kidnap locals. The regime said the gangs were rebels, while the rebels pointed their fingers at the regime. The rebellion had become far too close for comfort. Fighting also erupted in Douma and in Yarmouk.

Sometimes the shock waves from the bombs made the walls and the foundation of my family home and my siblings' houses shake. Mohammad's younger kids were aged three and five. Hivron's five kids ranged in age from fourteen-year-old Rawan to four-year-old Maya. Shireen's boys were aged eight, ten, and thirteen. Sometimes they had to flee their shaking homes and run to the local park, which wasn't exactly safe but at least no walls could crash down on them.

"The military is paranoid about people congregating in public,"

Hivron told me. "What if they mistake us for government protesters? And the rebels might think we are pro-regime supporters. Either way, we're a target. We're stuck in the middle of this crazy situation."

Picture your own city suddenly turning into a deadly war zone. Imagine being afraid to send your children to school. To go to work and back. To do even the most basic errands. Imagine what it would be like if your friendly neighbourhood suddenly turned hostile. For my family, it also became difficult to secure basic necessities like food and propane. Prices skyrocketed by as much as three hundred per cent, and so did the unemployment rate. The government started rationing the propane supply, allowing each family only one tank per month for six hundred lira. That price soon doubled and then tripled, and the vendors' prices also increased dramatically.

The city routinely experienced electricity cuts. Basic survival had become difficult for my family, though I didn't know just how bad things were at the time. People were becoming even more vulnerable to joining the fight. Gangs of unknown or questionable alliances began preying on the boys and men, saying, "Join us and we'll pay you enough money to feed your family." Or worse, "Join us or we'll shoot you and go to your house and burn it down." Violent kidnappings became routine. Citizens could no longer safely leave their homes, and they couldn't trust that they were safe at home. Even a brief conversation with a rebel or with a member of the regime could be misconstrued by the other side as sympathizing with the enemy. It became difficult to trust neighbours and friends, and a growing number of people were "disappeared": they simply vanished. One awful day, two of Ghouson's brothers, both young men in their twenties, disappeared. Her family had no clue whether they were taken by the secret police or by rebels, whether they were alive or dead. To this day, they still have no answers.

During this time, Hivron's thirteen-year-old son, Abdulrahman, and Mohammad's twelve-year-old son Shergo were playing soccer near the family home when a suicide bomber attacked, the shrapnel from his bomb—along with his flesh and bone—raining down onto my nephews. When Hivron took the boys to the hospital for treatment, they were bleeding and in shock. They were interrogated by security officials.

"Suddenly it's too dangerous for the boys to play soccer," said Abdullah. "You can't trust anything or anybody."

"Please consider moving back to Kobani, at least temporarily," I begged Baba when I spoke with him on the phone.

"*Hay souria. Bilad al-Sham.* This is Syria. Our city has survived for thousands of years," he responded. "It's the oldest living city in the world."

"But the whole country is shattering," I cried.

"Our country is the cradle of civilization," he countered. "It has survived many battles. Many occupiers. Many ethnic and sectarian clashes that tried to pit neighbours and friends and families against each other."

No matter what I said, my *baba* wouldn't be persuaded to leave. He seemed certain that the city would survive. But with the fighting happening all around my family's homes, it wasn't Sham's survival I was worried about.

قوي كالذئب

Qawee kal dhiʻb

Tough as a Wolf

By the middle of July 2012, more than one million Syrians had to flee their homes. The most feasible option for the displaced was to seek refuge in less dangerous areas within Syria. But too many regions had become dangerous, with hundreds of different rebel groups assuming control of cities, towns, and villages, and fighting against al-Assad's military forces. Some of these regions were called "liberated," meaning liberated from the regime. More often, it meant being liberated from food, water, electricity, schools, hospitals, and safe shelter. And if you happened to be a woman and your town had instituted ISIS's laws around proper dress, you were "liberated" from the freedom to leave your house without a *khimar* and an abaya, the face-covering veil and ankle-length robe. If you were Shia, Alawite, Kurdish, Armenian—name any ethnic or religious sect—you were "liberated" from the right to exist in your own country, unless you disowned your heritage and your beliefs. And if you were a Sunni Muslim who believed in secularism and ethnic and religious tolerance, you had to "liberate" yourself from liberal ideals.

Syrian citizens were caught in the middle of a civil war, which meant they had to pick a side or leave the country altogether. Many families fled to the border countries, including Lebanon to the west and Jordan in the south, or to the northern countries of Turkey and the Kurdish republic of Kurdistan to the northeast. All these countries had created refugee camps near border towns, though many families had to go to the big cities of Beirut and Istanbul to find work. When people started trickling into Lebanon and Turkey, they were not given legal work permits, and so they had to make a living in the underground economy, which made life very difficult.

Abdullah lived in Kobani, but he continued to commute to Sham for work. It was no easy task. The highway from Aleppo to Damascus straddled many territories under the control of various different rebel groups. One day, Abdullah was returning from Sham to Kobani. He was near Aleppo, inching ever closer to his home, when a group of long-bearded men seized him.

"You are a Kurd, and all Kurds are *kafreen*," they yelled, meaning, "You are not true Muslims." They spoke Arabic with the accents of foreigners. They got even angrier when they saw that Abdullah had a pack of cigarettes, which they considered حرام *haram*, forbidden. Then they accused him of being a Peshmerga fighter.

"Tell us about your next mission," they yelled. "Tell us where you're getting your weapons. Who are you getting them from?"

"والله, *Wallah,* I swear to God, I have no idea what you're talking about," Abdullah responded. "Yes, I am Kurdish, but I grew up in Sham, and I'm not involved with anyone."

But they didn't believe him. They dragged him to a nearby house that appeared abandoned. They took him to a room where four captive men dangled from ropes like sides of beef. They tied Abdullah up the same way. From the other rooms, he could hear men whimpering, or outright screaming in pain. The air was thick with the smell of sweat, urine, and blood, so intense that Abdullah started to vomit. Periodically, men would appear to beat and torture him: for being Kurdish, for having *haram* cigarettes, even for daring to fall asleep.

"Tell us the whereabouts of your comrades and your stockpile of weapons," they ordered.

"منشان الله, *Minshan Allah*. For the sake of God, I'm not a fighter. I'm just a barber with a wife and a baby boy," Abdullah said.

"Every Kurd is going to be killed," the terrorists continually reminded him.

After many days of beatings and torture, Abdullah began to wonder if he'd ever see his family again. After more than a week of this torture, the terrorists entered the room armed with pliers. They held open Abdullah's mouth and yanked out his teeth, one by one. It was so painful that Abdullah passed out at some point, flickering in and out of consciousness throughout the ordeal. When they finally finished, they left my brother with only the stumps of a few deeply rooted molars. He was living in a horror movie; no civil human being can even imagine it. Soon after, the terrorists concluded they had the wrong man. They threw him out and threatened that if he told anyone what had happened, they'd come after him and his loved ones.

It was the middle of the night. Abdullah stumbled down the road, walking for many hours, until a vehicle appeared. The plainclothes civilian inside took pity on him and drove him close to Kobani. When Rehanna saw him, she screamed.

"Shush," he whispered. Abdullah was so traumatized that he didn't dare tell anyone what had happened, except for close family. He was deeply scarred but relieved to be alive and back home with his family. He got antibiotics from a doctor, but he couldn't afford a dentist. His remaining broken teeth were useless; he often swallowed his food whole. His mouth was a festering wound, and the abscesses were hard to clear up. He lost so much weight that he looked like a skeleton.

Still, Abdullah's mind remained entirely preoccupied with finding work to put food on his family's table. He would never commute from Sham to Kobani again. So he decided to leave his wife and son and go to Turkey.

At first, Abdullah worked in Turkish towns near the border with Syria, doing whatever jobs he could find, like working at a warehouse and unloading produce from trucks. His body was still weak and his mouth was in a terrible state, but he tried his best to send money home to his family. He wasn't the only one facing challenges: there were many Syrians looking for work and many employers looking to exploit them. The typical wage was $7.50 per day. When Abdullah could no longer find work in the border towns, he went to Istanbul, a one-day's journey by bus from the border. There he picked up odd jobs in construction, sharing the rent on one room with ten other men, most of them Kurdish refugees who were also commuting between northern Syria and their jobs in Turkey. Abdullah tried to return home at least once every few months, and whenever any of the other refugees returned to Kobani, he sent money and food and whatever else he could scrape together for his family.

By March of 2013, the overall registered Syrian refugee count had reached 1.1 million. (That's equivalent to the entire population of Sham when I was a girl.) But that number is likely an underestimate. If Syrians didn't have a valid passport to enter another country legally, or they didn't cross through official borders, which was typical at the border with Turkey, they weren't counted. The refugee camps in Turkey, Jordan, Egypt, and Kurdistan had taken in over four hundred thousand Syrians. The camps offered basic survival, but many could not keep up with the steady flow of new arrivals. Some camps had inadequate sanitation and health care and were teaming with diseases and deadly parasites. The camp refugees also suffered from the invisible wounds of psychological trauma, from the stresses of living through warfare, to the indignities and humiliation that comes with being displaced. Registered refugees couldn't work; their movements in and out of the camps were restricted or disallowed altogether.

Meanwhile, life for my sisters Hivron and Shireen and my aged father in Damascus was even more unpredictable and fraught with danger. In the spring of 2013, the deadly terrorists with the long beards gave themselves a name: ISIS. The faction had already infiltrated many rebel groups, and they now claimed ownership of towns and cities in northern Syria, striking at their enemies throughout the country.

"So many people have fled to Sham that we don't know who our neighbours are anymore," my family told me when I called home.

Many residents of Sham had used up every penny of their savings, sold all their gold jewellery (for much less than the purchase prices), and liquidated every asset just to have enough food to eat, enough propane to cook meals, and enough *mazot* (diesel) to heat their homes. I was sending my family money for food, but the prices were sky-high. Like many other citizens, my family had to resort to burning their furniture just to cook and stay warm.

War changes people. There were lots of people ready to take advantage of the suffering: they would steal money and cars, loot shops, kidnap and kill people, rape girls. There was nothing *haram* anymore. Money and power became number one. People would say, "إن لم تكن ذئباً أكلتك الذئاب, If you are not a wolf, the wolves will eat you." There were very few people my family could trust.

I could often hear the sound of gunfire crackling in the background when I called Baba and my sisters. The local schools hadn't officially closed, but the teachers didn't always show up, and it had become too dangerous to let the kids go anywhere. The sight and sound of gunfire became routine. Bombs would explode, the shock waves killing full flocks of laughing doves, which rained down from the skies.

The war hadn't crushed my father's generosity, though. One day, he saw a family with young kids living in the park. He felt sorry for them and invited them to stay in his house. It wasn't long before his guests started to call more of their relatives to join them. Baba's house was like it was during my youth—a crowded hotel—but this time, it was filled with strangers. It eventually became too much, and Baba had to set limits, asking many people to leave. But that didn't mean he closed his heart or his doors completely. He took in a young widow named Duaa and her baby boy, Youssef, who was born with a severe learning disability. It gave me some comfort to know that Baba had a woman and child in his home, and that one thing hadn't changed: even in the midst of the destruction, my *baba* wanted nothing more than to cultivate a place in which love could grow.

PART

TWO

Chapter 6

آلان

Alan

Alan

Kobani was Rehanna's homeland, the place to which she returned to give birth to Ghalib in 2011, the place she fled to in 2012 after the fighting and suicide bombings in Damascus made life too dangerous, the place she remained while her husband shuttled back and forth to Istanbul to try to eke out a livelihood. Kobani was Rehanna's last safe haven.

Every day that he was working in Turkey, Abdullah was thinking about his wife and son. Rehanna was pregnant with Alan, and Abdullah couldn't wait to get back to Kobani to be with her. He returned safely before Alan was born, and I talked to them a few days before his birth.

"I'm going to explode," said Rehanna, laughing her lovely, contagious laugh. I had started calling her فرحانة, Farhana, which in Arabic means "happy and laughing."

"It's so hot—almost fifty degrees today—and this monkey inside is kicking me. Abdullah tries to put his ear to my stomach, but I have to move away before he gets kicked."

"What did you do today?" I asked her.

"We went to your dad's olive groves to clean up," she said. "They're so big, like me! I wish you could see them. I'll take a picture and send it to your dad; he'll be so proud."

Alan didn't come on his due date.

"This monkey is not coming out. I can't wait for that moment!" Abdullah texted.

Finally, Rehanna's contractions began. Abdullah called Rehanna's mom and my sister Maha, and they rushed Rehanna to the hospital in Kobani. The conditions at the hospital had degraded since the terrorists and the fighting had reached the surrounding regions. There was only one doctor there who could do a C-section. During the procedure, there were complications.

"Rehanna's heart almost stopped, and she had to be resuscitated," Abdullah said when I called for an update. "She lost so much blood and the hospital had a shortage of her type. But *Alhamdulillah,* everything was okay."

Abdullah stayed in the waiting room, according to Muslim tradition. He prayed and paced and pestered Maha each time she returned from the delivery room with updates.

"Maha, find out what's happening now," he demanded.

When she returned, she said, "ألف مبروك, *Alf mabrouk.* A thousand congratulations. You have another son!"

Abdullah and Rehanna's second son, Alan, was born on June 6, 2013, on the edge of one war zone and in the epicentre of another. Even in a war zone, the cycle of life persists.

When I finally got to talk with Abdullah, he was proudly holding his baby in his arms.

"حبيب قلبي, *Habib albi*. He is so tiny. ما شاء الله، مثل القمر, *Mashallah mitl al-qamar*, he's like a bright moon shining, so beautiful. Say something to your *ammeh*," he said, holding the phone near the baby's ear.

"Hello, my sweetheart. I can't wait to meet you," I said, my voice cracking.

"I swear, Fatima, he's smiling at you!" said Abdullah.

"How's Rehanna?" I asked.

"الحمد لله على سلامتها. Thank God for her safety, Rehanna is okay now."

Abdullah texted a photo of that precious baby. Alan had such light hair that I joked, "You're both so dark. Where did you get this boy? *Mashallah, mitl el mala'ekah*. He looks like an angel."

A few weeks later, Abdullah took his two boys to a local Internet cafe and we Skyped so that I could see Alan while I talked to him. He was tiny and he looked so peaceful sleeping in Abdullah's arms.

"This boy's an angel. He sleeps like a dream and when he's awake, he's such a peaceful, happy baby," Abdullah said. "I've never seen a newborn smile this much."

Ghalib wasn't smiling. He wasn't impressed.

"What do you think of your brother?" I asked him.

"He's a donkey. I don't like him," he replied. He looked at his dad and said, "Take him back to where you bought him from. How much did he cost?"

"One lira," joked Abdullah.

Ghalib considered this. "Okay," he said. "Let's go get our refund."

Our laughter woke up Alan, who started to coo like a dove.

"Did you choose a name?" I asked Abdullah.

"I'm shy, but I need to ask you something," he said. "Can I name him after your son? Can I call him آلان Alan? It's a beautiful Kurdish name, and Rehanna loves it too."

"Of course. It would be an honour."

After Alan was born, Rehanna's cheerful optimism prevailed, despite all the hardships of wartime life. When no water or food was available or the electricity was cut, she would say, "It's the perfect time to gaze at the stars and enjoy the moonlight: it's like a huge candle." Or when they had to use firewood to cook, she would say, "العصر الحجري, *Al-asr al-hajari*," meaning, "We are living in the Stone Age."

"She was a young woman in love," said Maha recently, when our talk turned, as it often does, to our dearly departed Rehanna and the boys. "She loved Abdullah to death. She was always telling him, 'Don't worry, the war will end and everything will be fine.' "

"She was a wonderful wife and a loving mother. She never complained about anything. She had hope for a brighter future," Abdullah often said.

Soon after Alan's birth, Abdullah had to return to work in Istanbul. He was saving every penny so that he could bring the family to Istanbul as soon as possible. Those goodbyes were always wrenching.

"Ghalib would always hold my hand so tight," Abdullah recalled to me later. "He would put the other hand up to Allah, and say, in a loud voice, 'الله يرزقك يا بابا, *Allah yerzaak ya Baba*. May God give more and more.' And when I got on the bus to leave, Ghalib would wave and call out, 'Bring us bananas when you come back, Baba.' And that would give me the strength I needed to persevere."

Soon after Alan's birth, the violence began to escalate across the country. The Syrian War had ravaged many cities in the western and southern provinces, including my dad's birthplace of Hama. Up to that point, with the Syrian forces battling the rebel groups in other parts of Syria, Kobani had been a calmer, safer place. That August, in the province of Aleppo, many people were massacred by ISIS and Al Qaeda's al-Nusra, including women and children. The terrorists then began to raid cities and villages closer to Kobani. Thousands of civilians had to flee their towns and villages. Some went to the city of Aleppo, others went to Kobani, and many others went to Turkey because it was the closest border country. People who stayed in the region increasingly risked being kidnapped, held for ransom, tortured, and beheaded. Rumours of increased warfare in the Aleppo region, in Idlib to the west, and Homs to the south, made travelling to Damascus a deadly prospect. The terrorists had the citizens of Kobani hemmed in.

A few months after Alan's birth, Rehanna and the boys left Kobani to join Abdullah in Turkey. The region was awash with terrorists, and they had to hire a smuggler to take them across the border. When their guide ordered everyone to walk in single file, they learned that the terrorists had placed land mines along the route. "Don't step out of the line," the guide barked. "Follow my path exactly." But at some point, a little girl did step out of the line and a mine exploded, maiming her legs. Luckily, Rehanna and the boys made it safely across that dangerous region.

Abdullah rented an apartment for the whole family for 400 lira per month—roughly $150 Canadian. He was working non-stop, making 650 lira per month, but it soon became impossible for them to afford the rent and feed a family on the remaining 250 lira per month. Regardless, life in Istanbul, free of the threat of daily violence, was something to be treasured.

Back in Syria, with autumn and the cold winter approaching and no end to that terrible war in sight, my siblings had to face the same choice that Rehanna had: remain in Syria and risk her life and the lives of her children, or flee to Turkey. My family and friends were living in a constant state of fear, wondering each and every morning, "If I leave the house to try to find food, will the house still be standing when I get back? Will my kids survive another day? Will I die and leave them orphaned?" Each and every night, they wondered, "Will I wake up tomorrow? And if I do, what's going to happen?"

Mohammad and Ghouson's family of six decided to flee to Kobani and then to Turkey because, among other reasons, Shergo, their twelve-year-old son, had a hernia. Only in Turkey would he have a chance of getting surgery. But land crossing had become perilous for grown men, never mind children. At that time, Mohammad's elder daughter, Heveen, was fourteen, their younger daughter, Ranim, was six, and their younger son, Rezan, only four. The family faced a chokehold of check-points and terrorists pouring in via the Turkish border, many of them from other nations. Yet these men had the gall to target Syrian citizens, calling them infidels for abandoning their country. The local Kurdish militia had closed all access roads to Kobani. Residents needed permission to exit the city.

Ghouson is not the average person; she is just as tough as my baby sister, Hivron, maybe more so. And she was willing to do anything to take care of her child.

"What would you do if your son was going to die?" she asked anyone who dared stand in her way. She had to spend the whole day at the city office, waiting for exit papers. She finally got what she wanted and returned home triumphantly.

The permission papers from the YPG, the Kurdish militia, allowed Mohammad's family to exit Kobani, but they still needed to cross a dangerous patchwork of land. As the family traversed the countryside toward the Turkish border, a group of rebels stopped them in their tracks. They seized Mohammad and beat him, calling him a Kurdish *kafer*, a rebel fighter and an infidel. Then they forced a rifle into Shergo's hand and ordered him to shoot his father.

"*Minshan Allah*, please don't do this," Ghouson begged, falling to her knees. "We're just a family trying to get to Turkey to get an operation for our son." She prayed until the terrorists took back the gun. They forced Mohammad to prove he was Muslim by reciting a line from the Koran. Finally, they let the family go.

"Mohammad could barely walk after that beating," Ghouson told me later. The family still had to get across a border crawling with Turkish police and smugglers, littered with land mines, and snared with barbed wire. They hid in a storm drain for hours alongside many other desperate citizens. When a man was stung by a scorpion and his arm had to be tied to stop the flow of potentially fatal venom to his heart, Mohammad and Ghouson made their move with their four kids. They found a gap in the barbed fencing, but each time a group of people got through, the guards in Turkey would fire their weapons into the air to scare the refugees as they chased after them. Eventually, Mohammad's family gathered the courage to sneak through the fence. Four-year-old Rezan was cut by the barbed wire and started to cry out in pain. Ghouson had to cover his mouth so as not to draw the attention of the police. When a group of Syrians ran across the field, they began to run too, but in a different direction. Shots rang out, but they kept moving. Finally, they came upon a farm owned by an elderly couple who took pity on them, saying, "The police will be following you. You can hide in our barn until they leave."

In that barn, among the sheep and goats, they hid under the hay and tried not to breathe while they listened for any sounds of approaching Turkish police. The seconds and minutes stretched out. Later, the couple returned to the barn with bandages for Rezan's and Mohammad's wounds, and water, bread, and jam.

Rezan told me his version of the story later, "Auntie, we hadn't had anything to drink or eat for two days, and I had a stomach ache from eating so much bread and jam." Ghouson added, "*Allah yikattir khairon. I pray for that good couple every day. They saved our lives.*"

Mohammad's family went to Istanbul and never looked back, except when they dared to dream of home. Sadly, his two youngest kids, Ranim and Rezan, took few memories of Syria with them, most of them stained by upheaval and violence. At first, the family stayed with a friend of Ghouson's in Istanbul, but they soon had to find their own place. Mohammad was still in pain from the terrorists' beating, but the UNHCR— the refugee agency meant to provide help and aid—was so overwhelmed by the flood of Syrians that Mohammad's family was turned away every time they tried to register for help. After a month or so, he got a job at a warehouse, loading boxes onto a truck. He met a Turkish man there who offered his family an apartment, but it was too expensive, so after a few months, they had to move again.

Back in Sham, Hivron had also been plotting her escape to Turkey. She had five children, including a teenaged son and three young daughters ranging in age from twelve to six. When the family finally left Damascus for Turkey, they had to say goodbye to Hivron's eldest daughter, Rawan, who was married by then and living with her mother-in-law, a disabled widow in a wheelchair. The goodbye was hard on everyone.

"Please stay safe," Hivron said to her daughter as she left. It was impossible not to wonder when, or even if, she'd ever see her eldest daughter again.

For the next few weeks, Hivron and her family traversed Syria, staying overnight in towns and villages with relatives and friends. They arrived in Turkey not long after Rehanna and the boys. Luckily, an apartment in Abdullah's building had become available, just above Abdullah's place. Both families were in a foreign world, but at least they had each other.

Baby Alan was three months old by then. "I'm holding Alan right now," Hivron said, when I called soon after their arrival. "He's sleeping like an angel. *Mashallah*. You need to see this boy in person. He will light up your life. And when he wakes up, he smiles and laughs. As soon as he's done breastfeeding, he falls right back to sleep. Lucky Rehanna—I wish my kids had been like that. But if they had, I'd want more babies, so maybe it's a good thing they weren't," she joked.

Ghalib's life was more difficult. He had a skin condition that had become painful and itchy. Abdullah took him to the doctor, who prescribed an ointment, but it was expensive—five lira for a small tube that lasted only one or two applications and didn't help much. Sometimes, the pharmacist would take pity on Abdullah and his family, giving him a free batch, but they couldn't count on that. The company of Ghalib's three cousins was a welcome distraction, and Hivron's only son, Abdulrahman, was a patient, loving babysitter for his younger sisters and the boys.

Money was tight for all my refugee siblings. Paying the rent was their chief concern and their biggest stress. I tried my best to help them with that. In 2013, I started working full-time again, taking a job at a franchise hair salon. I would send my paycheques to my siblings, and Rocco would help too, providing the lion's share of the money I sent to them. As long as my siblings could keep a roof over their heads, they could get by with a limited diet of stew and rice. Hivron also showed Rehanna how to make cheap, filling baby food for Alan by mixing milk with cornstarch and sugar.

"Do you have diapers?" I asked Rehanna one day.

"The disposable ones are too expensive. I use cloth diapers and cover them with plastic wrap." She never complained. Abdullah was the same. Once I was talking to him and he started calling out, "I see the paupers found us a treasure." He was talking to Hivron's kids, who had found a discarded couch on the street and had dragged it home.

At that time, Abdullah was working in a women's clothing sweatshop.

But even with the money I sent to my family and his salary, there was never enough to cover everything. After three months in the new apartment, Abdullah couldn't pay the rent on time. The landlord immediately evicted the entire family. Hivron's tiny apartment could barely contain her family of six, and she would have risked eviction too if she had also taken in Abdullah's family. Rehanna and the boys had no choice but to return to Kobani for the winter. They were going against a surge of Syrians seeking refuge in other countries. Media and aid organizations reported that Syrian refugees were so desperate to escape the war that they were attempting to seek asylum in Europe via smugglers' boats crossing the Mediterranean Sea to Greece and Italy, and some were drowning during the dangerous journey. Abdullah and Rehanna didn't want to consider that option; they still planned to find a new apartment in Istanbul so that the family could reunite once again. Every day was a struggle, but they refused to give up hope.

For Rehanna and the boys, life in Kobani was much more difficult that winter. The war had cut off the supply of water and electricity to the city. It got worse in the summer of 2014: though the city wasn't yet under direct attack from the terrorists, violence had reached the streets of Kobani. My dad's cousin was shopping in the local *souq* when a suicide bomber exploded and he was killed. Going about the business of daily life became increasingly dangerous.

Maha's husband, Ghalib, had previously made a living working at my uncle's car dealership in Aleppo, and in the summer months, he helped manage the grain and olive fields that his father had given him. But when Aleppo became too dangerous, their only source of income was a hardware store that Ghalib ran out of their house in Kobani. Their eldest son, Adnan, a plumber and electrician, had worked in Lebanon, but during a visit home he got stuck in Kobani; it became too dangerous to travel back to Lebanon. Now he and his dad spent their days in the shop, hoping for work to materialize.

One day, the father and son were sitting in front of the shop door when Maha called out, "Supper's ready!" so they came inside. Suddenly an explosion from a nearby suicide bomber cracked through the air, shattering all the windows of their house.

"If they had still been sitting out front, they would have been killed," said Maha. "الله ستر, *Allah satar,* I called them just in time. God protected them."

Kobani was becoming dangerous for all young men, just as Sham had been at the start of the war. Now only fighters had currency. Girls faced even grimmer options—like rape, sexual slavery, and forced marriage. Maha and Ghalib knew they had to get their family out of Kobani before it was too late. But to do so, they would have to split their family apart.

They sent Adnan and his eighteen-year-old brother Mahmoud over land to Izmit, a port city in Turkey about a hundred kilometres east of Istanbul, where some of Maha's friends had settled since escaping Syria. The rest of the family fled to Turkey soon after. As she abandoned her beautiful Kobani home, with the gardens she loved so dearly, Maha had no clue whether she'd see it ever again.

"When I looked at Mama's sewing machine, I broke down," Maha admitted. "When Mama was sick, she said, 'I want you to take it. But promise me you'll take care of it and pass it to one of your girls.' I felt like I was breaking my promise."

Maha worried they wouldn't survive the border crossing, so she hired a smuggler to assist them. The terrorists had gotten into the sinister habit of kidnapping young girls, and Maha wasn't taking any chances. She dressed her daughters in niqabs so their faces would be covered when crossing the ISIS-controlled checkpoint.

"We can't breathe," her daughters said.

"Be quiet. Keep your eyes down and your faces covered," Maha instructed as the driver's car inched closer to the guard's booth.

"Where are you going?" the border guard asked.

"I'm taking this family to the Turkish border," said the driver.

Maha and her kids kept silent, avoiding eye contact as the guard gave them a long, hard look.

Finally, he said, "Okay, go," and waved them through.

Maha and her daughters went to Izmit, where they reunited with her two sons. She lucked out on an apartment for three hundred lira per month. The kitchen and bathroom were shabby, but it had four bedrooms and was on the third floor, with a balcony that afforded them a view. They didn't have any furniture but found abandoned items on the streets. Adnan had found work in the plumbing and electrical field, but her sons-in-law had to take back-breaking jobs in construction. They came home after dark every night, collapsing onto the floor as soon as they entered the apartment. Maha would call out, "You're so dirty! Go straight to the shower." But even showering was work; they had to first boil water on the stove. "We're too tired," was their answer, and within minutes they would be fast asleep.

I continued to do what I could to help. I sent money to pay the rent for Maha, Mohammad, and Hivron, and sometimes I sent extra money for medicine or basic comforts, like electric hot water tanks so that they could take hot showers. But I couldn't wire money directly to my brothers and sisters through any official channels like banks or Western Union because claiming that money required valid passports. I had to send it through their Turkish neighbours or through friends, which was limiting and frustrating. All I wanted was to help my family; why was it so difficult?

As a refugee in Istanbul, my baby sister, Hivron, was eager to find work. She took her two youngest daughters for a walk in the neighbourhood and asked other Syrian refugees if they knew about employment opportunities. One family gave her the address of a potential employer, and she went straight to that location. A man was sitting on the stoop of a building.

"*Salam ya akhee,*" Hivron said. "Do you have any jobs available?"

"I do," he said. The man paused and examined Hivron and her daughters. "Come back tomorrow, and bring your kids."

Hivron could not believe her luck: it seemed she'd found a job and daycare, all in one.

"When I showed up at this place the next day, a minibus was pulling up, and a dozen little kids filed off," said Hivron. "I thought, 'Will I be working at a daycare?' We followed the kids inside and down the stairs to a dark, cold basement. A few machines were cranking out socks. Nearby, forty children worked, some as young as three years old. They were sitting on the dank tile floor with scissors, trimming the threads on the socks."

The man she'd met the previous day arrived and said to them, "You can get to work now. The kids will show you how to trim the socks."

"I realized I was so stupid," Hivron said. "That man expected my children to work. I was sick with rage, but I was too angry and shocked to say anything. I started working, and told my kids to do the same. As soon as that man went back upstairs, I talked to these tiny, dirty, starving sweatshop workers. Most were Syrian. One boy said, 'I'm from Aleppo. I lost my daddy.' Another one said, 'My mama is sick at home and we need to pay the rent.' But I said to myself, 'Shut up and investigate.'"

The man returned with their lunch—a pot of rice. "All those tiny kids rushed to that pot and started eating like starving puppies. When the man came back to collect the empty pot, the kids went like robots back to their work."

Hivron had seen enough.

"What kind of man does this to children? This is *haram*," she told the man. "You're not a human being. I will report you to the police." She took her kids home, and when Ahmad came home, she told him what had happened. Ahmad and Hivron decided they could not risk reporting the man to the authorities; it might mean they'd be deported. But that didn't quell their outrage. Ahmad marched over to the sweatshop and gave the man a piece of his mind.

Hivron got a job working in a fast-food restaurant that made barbecued chicken; her mouth watered and her stomach growled all day long. At closing time, all the leftover food was supposed to be discarded, but it was perfectly good, so Hivron often took it home for her family. One night, the manager caught her.

"Those chickens will make you sick," he said.

"I'll take the risk," she responded.

This new life was a shock to my family, just as it was to the many other Syrian refugees. When your life is turned upside down, when you have been forced to flee your home and leave everything behind, you do what you must to survive. In Syria, most of the women had never worked, but now, as refugees, they were forced to do so. Hivron didn't want her older kids to work; she wanted them to go to school. But she had the same problem that Mohammad and so many other refugees experienced when she tried to enrol her kids in classes. Hivron went to all the nearby schools, but the staff would say, "Our classrooms are full. Try again next year." Eventually, her son, Abdulrahman, got a job as a busboy at a restaurant, working nights, making twenty-five to forty Turkish lira per day—just fifteen Canadian dollars for up to twelve hours of work. Hivron was too worried for the safety of her teenaged daughter to let her work. She'd heard many horror stories about girls being sold or kidnapped to become wives or slaves, which was not unique to Turkey: it was happening everywhere, from Lebanon to Jordan to Syria.

The younger kids in my family had nothing to do all day. They had few toys and fewer books to read, most of them written in Turkish. The older children had to babysit their younger siblings while their parents worked—until they too took on jobs. Mohammad's two oldest kids, Heveen and Shergo, sometimes worked eighteen-hour shifts at a clothing factory, six days a week. Shergo's job involved pressing clothing with an industrial ironing press, and his arms were routinely burned as a result. Heveen's supervisor would threaten workers with a coat hanger. Heveen was so afraid of getting in trouble that if she had to go to the bathroom, she would hold it for hours so as not to risk abuse or, worse, be fired.

My family had managed to escape immediate violence in Syria. But finding safety in Turkey had brought new challenges, and their journey was far from over.

Chapter 7

هاي الحرب

Hay alharb

This Is What the War Has Done to Us

Refugees in Turkey had to endure many hardships and found it impossible to sustain even the most basic survival. But the situation in Syria was much worse. Abdullah was desperate to bring Rehanna and the boys back to Turkey. But with ISIS's chokehold on the region, her family had to plan their escape wisely and patiently. Abdullah was still working at the sweatshop, saving money so that he could rent someplace decent for his family when they arrived. He even asked his boss if he could sleep in the factory at night so that he wouldn't have to pay for a room. The boss took pity on him and agreed. Abdullah had Saturdays free, and he spent those days looking for a new home so that his family could join him as soon as possible. But with so many more refugees flooding into Turkey, it had become even more challenging to find somewhere to live.

I admit that I didn't fully understand these hardships until I saw them with my own eyes. I hadn't seen my family in more than three years, and I was desperate not just for a reunion but to meet my nephews Ghalib and Alan. I booked a trip to Turkey for five weeks starting in mid-August of 2014. I thought I might be able to fly my dad to Turkey, but my *baba* didn't have a passport, so he decided to risk taking the bus and go by land.

"That's far too dangerous, Baba, with those checkpoints everywhere, all those rebels and terrorists," I told him when I learned of his plan.

"What would the rebels want with me, an old man?" he responded. He asked my siblings what they were craving most from home. They unanimously agreed: Syrian coffee and baklava. Baba didn't have a lot of money to spare, but he brought just enough baklava so that everyone could have one piece. I called Baba the night before he left, and he shrugged off my concerns again, saying, "ما في حدا بيموت ناقص عمر, *Mafi hada bimout naqis omur.* Allah has already written everyone's time of death."

Baba took the route through the border town of Efreen, which lies east of Kobani, and was rumoured to offer the safest passage. It was a long week, waiting to hear from him. He had a cellphone, but there were often areas without a signal, places where none of us could reach him. Along the way, the bus stopped at many checkpoints, some under the command of rebels, some under government control, and still others guarded by the terrorists. Often, the terrorists would board the bus and interrogate the passengers, sometimes plucking men by the hair and dragging them off the vehicle. But as Baba predicted, they barely took notice of an old man. He made it safely to Turkey.

A few days later, I arrived in Istanbul. My dad, Mohammad, and

Abdullah met me at the airport. They all looked like old men. Even Abdullah's smile seemed old. I would find out exactly why soon enough. We went to Mohammad's house. It was after midnight, but Mohammad's kids woke up to see me and we stayed up all night. Over the next few weeks, my *baba* and I travelled back and forth between my siblings' houses, staying with each family for a few days at a time. It was a shock to see my baby sisters looking so old as well. Maha was forty-one and Hivron was only thirty-four, but the war had taken a toll. It had been more than three years since my last visit, and all my nieces and nephews had grown up so much—too much. Even the younger kids had a wise, wistful look in their eyes that no child should have. And they were so thin. Maha's daughter Fatima was eight months pregnant, but her bump was alarmingly small.

While I was there, I tried my best to help. But each time I looked at the faces of my family, I burned with shame for not sending them more money. I felt guilty when I hugged them and felt their sharp bones. I had always sent as much as I could afford, but my siblings were proud people and rarely asked for help—especially Abdullah.

Still, some things hadn't changed. The first time we sat down on the floor in Mohammad's house to eat a typical light meal of *labneh*, olives, cucumber, and pita, it felt just like the old days. Abdullah had become his former self again, making funny faces and pretending—or so I thought—to be an old man with no teeth.

"Baba, I want to eat cucumber. Can I borrow your dentures?" he mumbled, making us laugh until we cried. But after he'd finished playing the part, Abdullah wore a toothless grin.

"What happened to your teeth?" I asked him. He shrugged off my question with more jokes. But when the young kids went to play outside, he finally told me about his grim encounter with the terrorists.

That was just the first of many horror stories I heard in detail that night. We stayed up very late, my brothers and sisters-in-law and father filling my ears with hardships they and so many other refugees had endured. It was early morning when we finally went to bed. Mohammad had two bedrooms, but they only had one mattress. Abdullah, Baba, and I slept on rugs. I doubt I slept for more than a few hours that night, wondering, "How did this happen to my family? When will they be able to go home again?" In the late morning, my bones were aching. I'm sure Baba's were too, but he didn't complain. Neither did Abdullah. I took a quick shower—at least *I* thought it was quick. But when I came out of the bathroom, Mohammad was there, pointing at an invisible watch on his wrist.

"The bill for that shower will be so big," he said, and laughed.

I had another eye-opener when Ghouson, Shergo, and I went to the market and I bought some food for the big afternoon meal. On the way back, Ghouson stopped in her tracks beside a Dumpster.

"Look at that mattress. It's a good, clean mattress," she exclaimed.

"Are you crazy?" I asked. Ghouson was a clean freak, just like Mohammad.

"It's a good mattress," she repeated. "Shergo, let's carry it home. It's not even heavy."

When we got back, Ghouson and Heveen scrubbed and bleached the surface and then left it in the sun to dry. The kids were thrilled to have a mattress to share amongst themselves.

Imagine how our father felt, seeing his family living in such desperate situations. And it got worse when we went to stay at Hivron's apartment the following week. She was living on the third floor of a building that had been scorched by fire. The building should have been condemned, but why give it up when you are a slumlord who can take advantage of desperate refugees? When Baba and I walked up the flight of stairs to Hivron's apartment, I thought the building would collapse.

Everywhere I looked, the wood was burned black and rotting. It was the same inside her tiny one-bedroom apartment. The kids had to sleep on foam cushions in the living room.

Hivron's husband, Ahmad, insisted that I sleep with my sister on their one mattress, which took up the entire bedroom floor. They had access to a shared rooftop. It was so hot inside that Baba volunteered to sleep up there instead of in the apartment. "It's just like in Sham," he said, grabbing a foam cushion. Abdulrahman and Ahmad joined him. At night, it was very loud outside. I didn't get much sleep, and in the morning, I said to Hivron, "Maybe I should take Baba back to Mohammad's house."

Hivron's face crumpled. "You're ashamed of the way I live. You think I'm a dirty refugee." She started to cry. "هاي الحرب, *Hay alharb*. This is what the war has done to us."

"حبيبتي, *Habibti*. Sweetheart, I don't think that. Don't cry," I said, hugging her to my chest. "I know you're doing your best. I'm so proud of you. Of course we'll stay. Forget I mentioned it."

"It's not always so bad," she said, wiping her tears. "Sometimes I get decent tips at the hotel. The Saudi tourists are the best tippers. Once, a woman left me a whole bag of her clothes. I'll show you." She went to her suitcase and pulled out a few pieces of designer clothing and threw them on the bed.

"Remember how we used to get new clothes and shoes for Eid?" I said. "We used to put the shoes under our bed the night before and lay out our outfits."

"And we couldn't sleep because we were so excited to put them on."

We both started to laugh and cry all at once.

83

My dad was quiet during each visit to his children's temporary homes. He must have swallowed so many tears, picturing their former lives in Damascus, the family home, and the strong foundation of love and support that he had worked so hard to build for them. Of course, the most important thing was that all his children and grandchildren were alive, and we were together for the first time in far too long. Most of us, at least. Shireen and her kids were still in Damascus, and Rehanna and the boys were still in Kobani. Abdullah was desperate to be reunited with his family, and Baba was yearning to meet his youngest grandson, Alan, for the first time.

Cracks appeared on my father's brave face when the two of us left Hivron's early one morning to hunt for a decent cup of coffee. I convinced him that he could find such a thing at the nearby Starbucks. I ordered him an espresso.

"شو هاد, *Shoo haad?* What is this?" he asked, wincing after his first sip. "هاي مو قهوة, *Hay moo qahwah.* This is not coffee. It needs more than sugar to be any good." My father takes his coffee very seriously, but I knew that he was talking about so much more than coffee.

"I wish you would stay in Istanbul," I said. "We're so worried about you in Sham, so far from everyone. You could live with any of the kids. Or I could pay for you to get your own place."

"You and your brothers and sisters are already burdened enough. They don't need the extra expense of an old man. I'm going back home. بدّي موت بالشام, *Beddi mout bil Sham.* I will die in Sham. Or wherever I am when God decides it's time."

I did not want to think about that. "إن شاء الله العمر الطويل, *Inshallah al umar altaweel.* God willing you will live a long life," I said. But I was starting to understand that a refugee's life was in many ways just as brutal as life in a war zone.

"At least take my old iPhone," I said. "That way we can all keep in touch on WhatsApp."

Baba treated that phone like a creature from another planet. Even trying to answer a phone call was bewildering to him. Abdullah made it even worse when he prank-called Baba, disguising his voice and pretending to be one of Baba's friends in Sham. We sat in the other room, trying to hold our laughter, until the giggles burst from our lips.

"You and your technology can get lost!" Baba yelled at Abdullah.

On his Saturdays off, Abdullah took me and Baba to the flea market, where I shopped for clothes and toys for my nephews. Abdullah saw a bouzouki, an egg-shaped Middle Eastern lute, and he said, "Ghalib would love to play that. The boys love Kurdish music." I bought the bouzouki for the boys, among other things. When I helped Abdullah pick out a red T-shirt, jean shorts, and black sneakers for Alan, I thought nothing of their significance.

During that trip, I began to see the world through a refugee's eyes. You are there, wherever you happen to be, but you can't shake the feeling that life is going on without you. That you are a ghost among the living. We discovered that Istanbul has throngs of laughing doves just like Sham. They congregate in Taksim Square, and people love to feed them. But I felt as if I were looking at those birds through a telescope, as though I were far away.

I learned that this estranged state of mind is common to refugees. Everywhere I went, I talked to Syrians living on the streets and in the parks. Sometimes their children had to beg for food or sell tissues or sing to the crowds to earn a few coins. Syrian refugees had the same struggles in Lebanon, Jordan, Egypt—everywhere. It wasn't the exclusive fault of Istanbul or the country of Turkey and its many fine citizens. The government had many pressing concerns of its own. The people of Turkey, like the citizens of any country, had their own lives to worry about first and foremost. They didn't write the restrictive laws concerning asylum seekers, and they were also adversely impacted in many ways by the huge flood of refugees. Despite that, many people were very kind to my siblings.

When I visited Maha in Izmit, I was shocked to see that she had barely any furniture.

"Why don't you reach out to your neighbours for help?" I asked.

"I'm too ashamed يا أختي, *ekhti*, sister," she said.

I talked her into going to the cafe on the ground floor of her building to see if the locals might be willing to help out. Maha explained to the cafe owner that she was a Syrian refugee living upstairs and that she needed furnishings.

"I'll ask around," the man responded.

Within hours, a truck pulled up at Maha's house, filled with furniture.

Their Turkish neighbours were also generous during the holy Eid al-Adha, Feast of the Sacrifice. My brothers and sisters couldn't afford to uphold the tradition of giving meat to the poor and needy. They couldn't even afford to buy meat for themselves as an occasional treat. Some of their neighbours understood this, and when the time for Eid came, all my siblings received offerings.

"Did they bring lamb like in Syria?" I asked Hivron.

"Here, they bring cow meat. That beef was divine. It melted in our mouths. But it's another reminder that life has changed so much since the war. Remember when we were the ones helping the needy?"

War destroys lives. It leaves behind terrible wounds that turn into scars—on the flesh and in the mind. It also steals pride and dignity. And it steals the most from the people who can afford it the least.

One Saturday, we had a picnic just as we always used to do in Sham as kids. We went to a local park, spread a blanket on the grass, and barbecued some beef kebabs. While we prepared tea, we realized that we'd forgotten to bring sugar. There was another family picnicking nearby, so we sent little Rezan to ask if we could borrow a few spoonfuls of their sugar. He came back looking humiliated. They had waved him away like a beggar. The bias against Syrian refugees was even more apparent when I tried to find a home for Abdullah's family. I scoured every street for rental signs; some had signs that read "No Syrians."

Abdullah was worried that he wouldn't be able to find somewhere for Rehanna and the boys, and the situation in Kobani had gone from bad to worse.

"I couldn't go home for the last few months," Abdullah told me. In that time, the terrorists had inched ever closer to Kobani, bombing nearby towns and beheading citizens in the surrounding region as they closed in on the city itself. Now, it was not just small skirmishes or suicide bombers that threatened the citizens of Kobani; the city was under the threat of all-out war. The border crossings had become overwhelmed with more desperate people trying to get into Turkey. The situation got increasingly dangerous during my visit, and it became dire in mid-September 2014, when ISIS launched the Siege of Kobani.

ISIS tanks crushed many villages as they steamrolled toward the city, raping, murdering, mutilating, and beheading innocent civilians along the way. Their forces, numbering as many as five thousand, captured hundreds of villages surrounding Kobani, and the terrorists were leaning on the city from all three sides. We watched the news on TV and couldn't believe the images of Kobani residents fleeing their home and massing at the Turkish border.

Abdullah called Rehanna right away.

"What's going on? You need to get out as soon as possible," he told her.

"It's so scary," Rehanna said. "We're leaving in a few hours." She was rushing to finish packing. Alan was laughing in the background.

Rehanna left Kobani with her entire family as thousands of other residents and the neighbouring villagers also fled for their lives. We were on pins and needles watching the footage of the siege. The commentary was in Turkish, so I had to get the iPad and look at the Arabic and Western media coverage so that we could figure out what was going on.

"I'm so scared for my wife and kids. I need to go get them," Abdullah said.

"Don't be crazy," my dad responded. "Rehanna's father and her brothers are with her. They will get her and the kids across the border safely. Be patient. Maybe you can go to the border and wait for them?"

Abdullah asked his boss if he could take a few days off, but the boss told him it was too busy at work, and Abdullah couldn't give up his job if he wanted to put a roof above Rehanna and the boys' heads. Abdullah periodically called Rehanna on her cell, but she had no way to charge her phone, so conversations were brief.

"You can't look anyone you meet in the eyes because the terrorists are like wild animals," she told Abdullah.

There were so many threats facing Rehanna and the boys. Not only were the terrorists and checkpoints all around them, they also had to be wary of land mines. At one point, Rehanna tripped while carrying Alan and he hit his head. She had to carry him and keep him awake in case he had a concussion. Her arms ached. The boys were hungry, starving, and dehydrated. When they reached the border, thousands of desperate Syrians were there, yelling, "Please open the border!" and "Please give us some water!" The Turks wouldn't open the border, but eventually they threw water bottles over the fence.

I was due to leave Istanbul and fly back to Vancouver on September 20. I so wanted to meet Ghalib and Alan in the flesh, but the hours were ticking by, and they were still stuck at the border, with no sign of when they might get through.

Finally, on September 19, after ISIS had advanced to within fifteen kilometres of Kobani, the Turks opened the border. Rehanna, Ghalib, and Alan were among sixty thousand Syrians that managed to cross and make it into Turkey. The majority of Rehanna's family stayed near the border; they planned to go back to Kobani as soon as they possibly could. As I was boarding the plane to return to Vancouver, Rehanna, Ghalib, and Alan were boarding a bus and settling in for the day's travel to Istanbul. I missed seeing them by a handful of hours. I should have changed my flight, but I had spent so much money already, providing each of my siblings with rent and necessities. *It's okay*, I told myself. *They are safe now. And you'll see them when you visit next summer.*

When I arrived home in Vancouver, I called Abdullah.

"I'm in heaven," he said. "My family is with me. We're together, and I have the whole world."

"Did you find a place to rent?" I asked Abdullah.

"Not yet. We're still looking, الله ما بينسى حدا, *Allah ma biyinsa hada.* God won't forget anyone. We're staying with Rehanna's friends for now."

I found out much later that they weren't actually staying with friends. They were staying with Mohammad and Hivron. Both of my siblings knew they couldn't host the family for long: if their landlords found out, they'd be evicted. Abdullah had nowhere else to turn but to his boss at the clothing factory, asking if his family could stay in the factory during the night. "I promise it's only temporary, until I find a place."

His boss took pity and agreed. The family slept beside the workers' toilet and day kitchen. The boss's wife offered them foam mattresses and pillows, and for blankets, they used old cloth they found at the factory. In the early mornings, the family would roll up their bedding and personal items and stow them away. Rehanna and the boys spent the days in a nearby park while Abdullah worked. When work ended at seven p.m., Abdullah rushed to collect his family and bring them back to the factory. After a week's time, one of Mohammad's neighbours got in touch with them and told Ghouson about a potential rental property.

"I have a sort of studio apartment next door to the building where I live," the woman told Abdullah. "It's unfinished, but it has a Turkish toilet, a faucet, and electricity. I'm using it as a storage place right now, but I'll rent it to you, as long as you take responsibility for clearing it out and setting it up."

Abdullah gratefully accepted. He and Mohammad got to work hauling away the junk. When Rehanna and the boys moved in, there was a plaid couch, a mattress frame, a broken TV, a faucet sticking out of the wall, and the Turkish toilet, which was basically a tile slab with a plumbed hole in the middle. To say that it was less than ideal would be too kind to that "studio apartment," but Abdullah and Rehanna didn't care. They were in their own nest, the whole family under one roof.

Abdullah got an inflatable children's pool and put it beneath the faucet so the boys could have a place to play and bathe. He kept his eye out for abandoned items on the streets of Istanbul. He soon found a decent mattress and some toys—a tricycle, a dump truck, little plastic cars, and some stuffed animals. He purchased a portable propane stove with one burner—the sort you might take on a camping trip—to cook with. Later, Abdullah had the broken TV repaired so that his boys could watch cartoons. Abdullah sent me some videos of the family in their new home. One was of the boys bathing in their inflatable "tub." Alan sat in one corner, splashing and giggling, while Ghalib circled around him, saying "Move, Alan, move."

"Careful, Ghalib. Mind your brother," Abdullah said.

Alan splashed and splashed. That boy loved to be in the water.

Another video featured Ghalib strumming the bouzouki I'd bought him in the bazaar. And when he heard his favourite song—"Shamame" by Ibrahim Tatlises—he would make everyone stop what they were doing to join hands and dance around in a circle like Kurdish dancers. Alan would jump around through the entire song, clapping and laughing. Alan couldn't pronounce all the lyrics—all he could say was *"mame"*— but he would sing it at the chorus with everyone else. Rehanna loved to sing too. "We are a family of musicians," she said. "You don't need instruments when you have a voice."

I imagine that if you stood outside that family's happy little house, closed your eyes, and listened, you would have had no idea that they were poor refugees barely surviving.

"When are you coming to visit us, عمة, *Ammeh*, Auntie?" Ghalib asked me in one of our regular Skype calls.

"*Inshallah, habibi.* I hope to visit soon. Or maybe you will come to Canada; it's beautiful here."

"Do you have candy there, Auntie? I like nougat."

"Yes, but the best candies are in Sham, at Souq Al-Buzuriyah."

"Ghalib and Alan would love that," said Abdullah. "Remember how they made candies right in front of our eyes and we were drooling while we waited?"

"My mouth is watering just thinking about the *mlabbas*," I said.

"*Inshallah,* we'll be able to take them there one day with our *baba,*" Abdullah replied.

Abdullah's commute to the clothing factory was long—two hours each way. In the mornings, his kids would wake him up, smothering him with hugs and kisses, which fortified him for another grueling day of work. And as soon as he opened the door upon returning home, the hardships of the day vanished.

One morning, they woke up to the sound of meowing outside. When they opened the door, a skinny black-and-white cat was looking up at them. Little Alan started laughing and clapping and groping at that cat with his hands. Surprisingly, the cat didn't seem to mind.

"He looks hungry. Can we feed him?" asked Ghalib.

Abdullah let the cat in and gave her some of their breakfast, after which the cat curled up on the couch and fell fast asleep. She became the fifth member of the family. They called her *Pisikeh*, Kurdish for "cat."

"Do you feed the cat milk or cat food?" I asked Rehanna when I called one afternoon.

She laughed. "She gets whatever we're eating."

"What are you eating tonight?" asked this nosy sister-in-law.

"I'm making a lentil stew and rice."

"How can you do that with only one burner?"

Rehanna laughed again. "It takes longer, but it's no problem. The boys love rice with yogurt, so I make a pot of that every day too."

"Maybe you can buy a real stove one day."

Her reply was classic Rehanna and typical of her continued optimism about returning home: "Why would I need a new stove? I already have a nice one in Kobani."

Abdullah's family got out of Kobani just in time. Many other citizens weren't so lucky. By early October 2014, ISIS had control of much of the city. For the next few months, deadly battles continued on the city streets, but the allied forces—Iraqi Kurds, Turkish Kurds, the

Americans—continually gained ground. By January 2015, they had re-gained control of much of Kobani, and by month's end, ISIS admitted defeat and fled, though they vowed to return and seek vengeance. They were true to their word. The citizens who returned to Kobani in June of that year, during Ramadan of all times, would face another ISIS on-slaught.

Many of our close relatives—fifteen in total—were massacred during those Ramadan attacks in June 2015. My family sent me photographs of citizens who had been beheaded by ISIS. One of them was Mary, my *baba*'s cousin. She was up early one day during Ramadan when she heard a commotion. She went outside. Terrorists were waiting for her with machetes. Her screams woke her two sons, who rushed out of the house. All three were beheaded. Other relatives from Aleppo who had fled to Kobani met a similar fate. One was blown up by a suicide bomb that left him recognizable only by the ring on his finger.

"Rehanna is shattered," Abdullah said when I called him in Istan-bul. "What kind of men slaughter children and kill innocent people? It's *haram* to do such evil things. Where is the morality? There is no religion anymore. Only greed for power and money."

Kobani and surrounding villages were devastated by the siege and its aftermath. All the critical infrastructure was destroyed. Rehanna's family home was hit by bombs and sniper bullets, but somehow it remained standing; many other homes and businesses were flattened. My sister Maha's house was destroyed, and so was the adjacent house she had built for her sons and their future families. The dream that she might one day return to her home had become nothing more than that—a fantasy that lived only in her mind.

"Any of our possessions that survived were stolen," Maha later told me. "Probably Mama's sewing machine too."

My *baba*'s trees of fat olives in Kobani—the ones that he had inherited from his father many years before the war—were gone too. We heard that ISIS had burned our olive orchard to the ground and destroyed our little property. When I spoke with my father back in our family home in Damascus, he said, "It's like my heart has been scorched." But then he continued, "الشجر بينزرع وبيرجع, *Al-shajar beynzra' w berja'*, Trees can always be replanted."

Chapter 8

الله كريم، بتهون

Allah karim, bithoon

God Willing, It Will Get Easier

My trip to Turkey changed me. As soon as I returned home in late September 2014, my first priority was to attempt to get my siblings asylum in Canada. But to do that, I would have to navigate the bewildering bureaucratic asylum-seeking process. The Canadian government had granted asylum to only 1,002 Syrian refugees since July 2013. Prime Minister Stephen Harper had a vague plan to allow about 11,000 Syrians to seek asylum in Canada over the next few years. Despite these plans, the Harper government had what seemed to me an indifferent attitude to their plight.

I wanted to bring both of my brothers and their families to Canada. Mohammad's wife, Ghouson, was pregnant, and they had four school-aged children who had fallen years behind in their schooling. Shergo and

Heveen were still working at the clothing factory; their teenage years had been stolen from them, and it seemed as if their young adult lives would be just as grim and hopeless as their adolescence. Those kids were smart, honorable, and hard-working, just like their parents. Shergo was becoming a handsome young man, and Heveen was a beautiful young woman, constantly eyed by men looking to marry a young Syrian refugee, even though she wore the hijab to cover her long curls every time she left the house.

I would have liked to rescue all my siblings from their dismal lives. But the majority of refugees that were granted asylum in Canada came from private sponsorships from citizens, which cost $28,000 for just one family of six. The government rarely funded refugees, and even with private sponsorships, approval by the Canadian government also required approval from the Turkish government and the UNHCR, which involved intensive, slow vetting. We couldn't possibly afford to sponsor all five families by ourselves.

Shireen's husband had an income selling falafels in Sham, and so did Hivron's husband, though it was meagre. Maha's husband could also work, and they had adult kids helping generate income, at least. So I focused my initial efforts on my two brothers, who needed more help. If I managed to bring them to Canada, Mohammad's family would live in my house, and my sister-in-law, Rocco's sister, Anna, who lives in Toronto, would host Abdullah's family at her house.

"If Anna can do this for my family, I will be grateful forever," said Abdullah when I told him our plans.

Anna was an incredible help. I knew nothing about the immigration process; I didn't know how to start. Anna researched the steps, and every time she found new information, she called to explain it to me. The best option was to go through one of the many sponsorship agreement holders (SAHs) in Canada that were attempting to help refugees with asylum and resettlement in Canada through private sponsorships. The majority of the SAHs were religious groups of many different denominations, from Anglican to Muslim, or community-based charity groups. These churches and groups would say, "Send us the necessary application forms and the required sponsorship money, and we will try to help you."

For three months, every single day, Anna and I reached out to many organizations in Toronto and Vancouver. With the help of my neighbour Kitt, we filled out all the necessary forms. The applications required detailed information from each member of Mohammad's and Abdullah's families, including my brothers' military records and the names of every school they had ever attended. They also required specific passport-style photos and original identification, all of which my brothers sent to me. But we discovered that the Canadian government also required a valid Turkish residence permit, called a *mavi kimlik*, for each family member. The residence permit was impossible for refugees to get because Turkey did not grant them to citizens of non-EU countries. The only identity card that the Turkish government issued refugees was a *yabanci* card. All my siblings got the *yabanci* card when they entered Turkey, but it didn't mean much to the Canadian government. Syrian refugees who had made it to Turkey were still officially considered illegal, whether they had a *yabanci* card or not. They could not legally exit the country; they could not access work permits or even receive much humanitarian aid, at least until October 2014, when the restrictions relaxed a bit.

Canada also required a valid passport for each family member, which was problematic. Of my family members, only Hivron had a valid passport. Maha and her family didn't even have expired passports, and neither did Rehanna, Ghalib, Alan, and a number of my younger nieces and nephews. It was next to impossible for refugees to renew their passports at international embassies outside of Syria. This lack of a valid passport was the main roadblock for my family and millions of other Syrian refugees.

Mohammad and Abdullah spent hundreds of lira that they couldn't afford just to try to fulfill the Canadian government's requirements. The applications required original signatures, so I had to send pages of the paperwork to my brothers in Istanbul, which then had to be routed back to me. I drove my family half crazy with requests for impossible paperwork. Every time I thought that I had things under control, I'd find there was another step or another document missing.

"We can't get the papers that Canada wants," Abdullah told me. "You and Anna and Kitt are doing your best to help us, we know. But it seems that the world will only recognize us as human beings if we have the right papers, which are impossible to get."

Still, we were determined to keep trying. We kept contacting the SAHs. I must have reached out to every church in Canada. Every single day, I was begging for help, but each step I took seemed to take me ten steps backward. It was a terrible time of my life. Day after day, the answer was the same: "We're sorry, but the government's requirements are impossible for most refugees to get. We can't help your family."

We were not looking for what some critics of refugee relocation call "a free ride." Rocco and I were committed to providing the entire $28,000 the government required for private sponsorship of Mohammad's family. In the end, we did submit an application for Mohammad's family, and I planned to do the same for Abdullah's family when I had saved enough money for a second application. I knew the paperwork was incomplete, but I was so angry and frustrated with the bureaucracy that I wanted to challenge the government's smothering requirements.

There was one other way of receiving the Canadian government's approval, which required another document in lieu of an exit visa or valid passport: an official referral from the UNHCR, the UN's refugee agency. This UNHCR approval was a maddeningly elusive thing. Mohammad had first registered in 2013; in 2014, Abdullah and Hivron tried many times to get that UNHCR referral, joining the throngs of other refugees in the long lineups at the UN office, waiting for hours, inching ever closer to the front of the line, only to be turned away when the offices closed.

I emailed the UN offices in Ankara and wrote about Mohammad's and Abdullah's families' predicaments, from the lack of schooling to the slave labour to their many medical issues, including Ghouson's difficult pregnancy, Ghalib's skin condition, Abdullah's abscessed mouth, and the overall desperate state of affairs in Istanbul. I got no response. When Ghouson suffered a miscarriage, I emailed the UN again and begged an employee to call my brothers and find some way to help them.

My family members didn't hold their breath waiting for a call from the UN. Through the grapevine, they had heard hundreds of stories about people unable to get UN approval. It seemed that there was nowhere left to turn.

By December, work had slowed down at the clothing factory where Abdullah worked. He had to take whatever jobs he could find in construction, sometimes working twelve-hour days, just to make enough money to scrape by. Often he had to travel by bus for many hours, leaving before the kids woke up and returning after they'd gone to bed. Finally, that December, a man from the UN actually called Abdullah. Abdullah gave the man a brief account of their hardships, and the good-hearted man empathized.

"We're going to help you," he said. "Where would you like to re-settle? Germany? Sweden?" Abdullah couldn't believe his ears.

"I don't care where, as long as we can get help and my kids can have a health treatment, a better future."

The man set up an appointment for Abdullah at the UN office in Istanbul two weeks later. That phone conversation gave him such hope. When I talked to him, he was flying high.

"Tima, I know you're trying to bring us to Canada. But it's clear that your government doesn't want us. If we can get to Europe, we have to try."

Two weeks later, Abdullah brought Ghalib to the appointment at the UNHCR, but they were forced to wait all day in a lineup with many other desperate refugees. Eventually, a UN staffer announced to the crowd, "The office is about to close. Come back tomorrow."

"But I have an appointment!" Abdullah called out. The worker waved him into an office. She looked at the skinny-boned father and son, saw Ghalib's angry skin condition, and listened to his terrible cough. She said she would help them immediately. She couldn't provide UN approval on the spot; she admitted that the process might take a long time because it needed to be evaluated both within the UNHCR and by the Turkish government. She told Abdullah that she would send his file to their head office in Ankara, and handed him a piece of paper with the date of his next appointment—more than a year later. That winter, Hivron also got a date for her first UNHCR interview, which was scheduled for September 27, 2016, over a year and a half later. The only immediate help that the Istanbul UN worker provided Abdullah was the address of a doctor to treat Ghalib's skin and an address for him to access food donations. The next day, Abdullah spent the last coins in his pocket to reach the food bank.

"It was like a zoo of ants," Abdullah said, describing the number of refugees waiting in that lineup. He didn't make it to the front that day, so he left empty-handed. The next morning, he travelled for hours to begin the process all over again. After many more hours, he got to the front of

My *baba*, my mama, my sister Hivron, and my uncle Khalid on Mother's Day with a cake that Uncle Khalid made.

Me *(left)*, Maha, my uncle Mahmoud, baby Abdullah, and my *baba* gathered in our family living room. Maha and I are wearing matching dresses that my mama made for us.

Shireen, Hivron, and Mama at a park in Damascus.

Blowing out the candles on my birthday cake during a party at my family's home in Damascus. My favourite song at the time was "Rasputin" by Boney M.

My mama and I celebrate New Year's at my uncle Mahmoud's house. Singing and dancing with family at home was typical on so many of my nights growing up.

Here I am visiting Maha's house in Kobani. My hair says it's the 1980s.

Taking a break at Lina's hair salon in Damascus in 1990. The salon was called Sandra—Lina's favourite Western name.

I was pregnant with Alan when I posed for this photo by the waterfront in Vancouver in January 1993. My son was born just three months later.

My first job in Vancouver was working the overnight shift on the local newspaper's printing press. Many of my co-workers were also immigrants, from the Philippines, India, and Pakistan.

From left to right: My sisters Shireen and Hivron; my son, Alan; and Baba and Mama gathered on the rooftop of our house in Damascus in 1994. It was my first trip back to Syria after leaving, and I couldn't wait for my son, Alan, to meet his family.

My brother Abdullah and my son, Alan, visit for the first time in our parents' living room in Damascus in 1994.

My brother Abdullah horsing around with our family in 2011. *From left to right:* Yasser and Maleek *(on shoulders)*, Abdullah and Maya *(on shoulders)*, and Abdulrahman and Noor *(on shoulders)*.

I got to visit with so much of my family in 2011, my last trip back to Damascus. *Front row, from left to right:* Ghoufran, Maya, and Maleek. *Second row, from left to right:* Abdulrahman and Yasser. *Third row, from left to right:* Hivron, me, Shireen, and Rehanna. *Top row, from left to right:* Noor, Rawan, and Heveen.

Rehanna and Abdullah took this photo with Ghalib for Eid in 2011.

Abdullah standing with Alan and Ghalib in front of their house in Istanbul in July 2015. Alan was always smiling.

Top: Alan *(left)* and Ghalib *(right)* on their couch at home in Istanbul, cuddling one of their favourite toys. *Lower left:* Alan in Istanbul during Eid in July 2015. *Lower right:* Ghalib and Alan crossing the Bosphorus in Turkey on a ferry during Eid in July 2015.

Much had changed when Abdullah returned to Kobani in October 2015, forty days after the tragedy. Here he is standing in front of the remains of his neighbour's home.

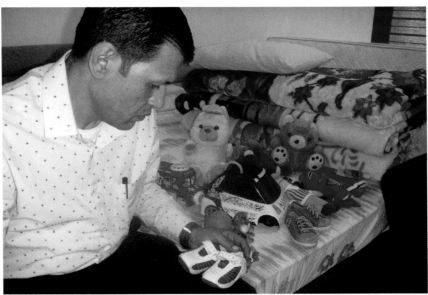

Abdullah, in his house in Erbil, is holding a pair of Alan's shoes. The toys that Abdullah managed to save are on the bed around him.

This welcome sign for refugees was on display in Brussels just a few days after the tragedy. It was a sign of things to come—I later delivered a petition to the United Nations High Commissioner for Refugees with one million signatures from people who welcomed refugees.

Abdullah and I handing out donations at a refugee camp in Kurdistan in 2016. Helping children in the refugee camps was the only thing that could bring Abdullah joy after the tragedy.

Abdullah and I on an overlook above a refugee camp in Kurdistan.

My *baba* resting at home in Damascus in 2016. Beside him is the framed photo of my mama that kept us company after she died. We would sometimes talk to her during our meals to remind ourselves of her presence.

I was invited to a town hall in Vancouver in December 2015, where I asked Prime Minister Justin Trudeau what Canada could do to help bring about a peaceful solution that would end the war in Syria.

I was so proud when my nephew Rezan and my niece Ranim started at their new school in Vancouver.

After Abdullah moved to Erbil, Kurdistan, in 2015, he was greeted by Masoud Bar-zani, the president of Kurdistan.

In February 2017, Representative Tulsi Gabbard *(right)* invited me to Washington, DC, where I spoke to reporters about my family's experiences and tried to convey the hardships that refugees face around the world. Representative Tom Garrett, Jr. *(far left)*, and Representative Peter Welch *(second from left)* also attended the speech.

ALAN KURDI

June 6, 2013–September 2, 2015

الله يرحمه.

Allah yerhamo

Rest in peace

the line. For his troubles, he was given a package of spaghetti, a bag of lentils, and some sugar.

"You can go to another location for cooked food," said a worker at the food bank. Off Abdullah went to another address, where he joined another lineup of desperate people. After waiting for hours, not going to work, and spending precious money on bus fare, Abdullah got to the front of the line, where he was served a single plate of spaghetti with tomato sauce.

"*Alhamdulillah* for the food," Abdullah thought.

By New Year's Eve of 2015, Anna and I had exhausted every possibility with our government. My family still didn't have even one of the three essential documents required by the Canadian government. The last thing I wanted to do was celebrate. I think I would have traded anything to be back in Sham, having a huge meal with my family, which always began with a prayer and a toast: "May God bless everyone around the world, and let us return to this table together for the next hundred years." As kids, after our New Year's meal, we'd run up to the roof to do the countdown and watch the annual fireworks that lit up the skies. Now, our city of jasmine was in total darkness because of electricity shortages; it had been an unseasonably cold winter, and the only things lighting up the skies that night were mortar and rocket shells. My *baba* never mentioned the situation when we spoke on the phone. But that night, he was feeling lonely and disheartened.

"People are losing hope that this war is ever going to end," he said. "*Inshallah*, one day, we will rebuild this broken country and my grandkids will have a future in Syria. I'm glad I can see the kids sometimes on video, but it's not the same. I'm missing so much. Even with Abdullah, who talks non-stop about his kids. As soon as I answer the phone, he says, 'Baba, talk to Ghalib,' and hands the phone to Ghalib, who starts chatting to me in Kurdish. I never get a chance to ask Abdullah how *he's* doing. He just says, 'I'm in heaven because I'm with my kids. You should see Ghalib playing the bouzouki; Alan can understand everything I say in Arabic and everything Rehanna says in Kurdish, and he even understands Turkish.' I've never seen a father who cares as much about his kids as Abdullah. Your mom would be so proud."

That phone call made me feel as if it had been one hundred years since I'd spent the holidays with my family. We were a long way from our childhood celebrations. Now my siblings could barely afford a decent meal.

"Are you making anything special for the new year?" I asked Abdullah when I called him that night.

"I got Rehanna and Ghalib a special treat: canned sardines," said Abdullah.

"I would do anything for Mama's kibbeh."

"Don't remind me. My mouth is watering thinking about it," Abdullah said. "Don't worry, أختي, *ekhti*, sister. الله كريم، بتهون, *Allah karim, bithoon*. God willing, it will get easier. Enjoy your family."

I tried to take Abdullah's advice. That night, Rocco convinced me to go over to our neighbours' house, where they were having a small party. But I couldn't think about anything other than my family. I told my friends that the only option I had left was a "Group of Five"— a five-party private sponsorship. But I wasn't convinced it would work.

"How will I get a group together?" I asked.

"I'll put my name forward," said my beautiful neighbour Kitt.

Another one of my neighbours volunteered to help. Rocco said he would chip in too. And then there was me. We needed just one other member for our G-5.

A few days later, I was at the salon where I was working at that time. I mentioned our plan to a client and friend named Claire.

"Mike and I would love to help your family," said Claire. "Count us as number five."

I was amazed. In just a few days, I suddenly had a team! But there was still much work to be done. The G-5 required much more paperwork. Without help from Kitt, I don't think I could have filled out any of those forms. But if my people could somehow survive that war, I could survive a blizzard of paperwork. We decided to sponsor Mohammad's family first, and I also got paperwork for Abdullah's family so that my sister-in-law Anna could put together a G-5 for him. But one day, Anna called me with bad news.

"Tima, I've been reading through the paperwork," Anna said. "Even the Group of Five process requires your family to have a *mavi kimlik* and a valid passport."

"What? I thought the G-5 would avoid that."

"I'm afraid not. The government still needs that ID, no matter what."

I was heartbroken. Once again, I had hit a dead end.

But then Anna had a brilliant idea. "Why don't you talk with your local MP and see if they can help?" she suggested.

So, Kitt and I contacted Fin Donnelly of the New Democrat Party, my local Member of Parliament, to discuss the Canadian government's near-impossible requirements. We set up an appointment to visit Fin at his office. I told him about my family's situation. Fin and his assistant, Karin, were deeply saddened and concerned.

"I will stand up for you. I will try my best to help get your family to Canada," he said.

"Can you deliver a letter from Tima to Chris Alexander?" Kitt asked Fin. Alexander was the Minister of Citizenship and Immigration, and he could have a lot of influence.

"I'm going in a few days to Ottawa. Send me your letter, and I'll make sure your letter is hand-delivered to him, or at least to his office."

I wrote that letter from the heart, with my tears running down my face. I described the general hardships of my refugee family and explained that the government's requirements were impossible for my family to meet. Fin, true to his word, delivered my letter to Chris Alexander. I heard nothing from the immigration office, so we continued to fill out the G-5 paperwork. When I told my family about my meeting and the letter, I was shocked by their response.

"خلاص، أختي, *Ekhti, khalas.* Enough, sister. It won't work. Canada just isn't an option for us," said Abdullah.

By the end of April, I was lost. "Everybody is telling me I'm wasting my time," I said to Rocco.

"Let's send the application anyway," he said. "I read on the government website that if they reject a claim, we can appeal it in court."

So I persevered. But I was beginning to understand why refugees were risking their lives to make dangerous crossings to get asylum in Europe rather than try to reach North America. By the start of that winter, more than 200,000 refugees had fled to Europe, and 3,500 had died or gone missing attempting to reach Europe, the majority perishing while crossing the Mediterranean.

Even the weather wasn't on the refugees' side that winter. It was unseasonably cold and snowy in Syria, in Turkey, and across the Middle East. Mohammad and Abdullah took whatever temporary jobs they could find with many different construction companies. One job involved twelve hours a day of digging in the frozen dirt and mud.

"Why pay for mechanical diggers when you have Syrian animals that will do the work for next-to-no pay?" my brothers lamented. Once the digging was done, the concrete work began, which was just as difficult. Mohammad was lucky to have a *sobia* in his apartment, a small wood-burning fireplace to provide heat. Wood and charcoal were very expensive, and they had to use it sparingly. The Turkish government provided refugees with some free charcoal, but it was never enough. Abdullah's little place didn't have any source of heating; the propane stove was strictly for cooking. But the landlord had come to love the family, and the family called her Teyze, which is Turkish for Auntie. She gave the family a wood-burning stove and let Abdullah cut a hole in the wall so that the fireplace flume could vent outside. When Abdullah couldn't afford to buy charcoal, he would get on his bike and scavenge the city for wood. But when he burned wood, his neighbours in the adjacent apartment building got upset.

"Your smoke is stinking up our laundry," they would bellow.

Each time this happened, Abdullah's blessed landlord Teyze came flying down the stairs.

"Shame on you!" she'd yell. "It's cold. They've got two little boys. What option do they have?" It was true: what else could Abdullah do?

It remained hard for Abdullah to leave his little house every morning to go out and face another long, cold day at a construction site. But his beautiful kids were his alarm clock.

"Go tickle Baba and wake him up," Ghalib would whisper in Alan's ear. "Bite him."

Alan did whatever his big brother asked.

"The tickling was nice. But Alan was growing sharp little teeth," Abdullah told me later.

Before he left for work, he would get down on his hands and knees and his boys would climb onto his back to play their game of shepherd transporting two lambs.

"يا غنماتي, *Ya ghanamati*. My beloved lambs," Abdullah would sing.

"ماء، ماء, Maa, maa," the boys bleated.

"انتو حياتي، شو طعميكن, *Into hayati, shu-ta'amikon*. You are my life. What should I feed you?"

"Cookies!" Ghalib would shout. "Can you bring me cookies to-night?"

"I will bring you a treat."

Back in Vancouver, I continued my quest to get the government to approve my private sponsorship of Mohammad's family. Rocco and I also wanted to help out with Anna's sponsorship of Abdullah's family once we had his application ready. And we were also paying for our own son Alan's education: a business degree at a local college.

My son had worked part-time since the age of sixteen, and he always paid for all his own personal things, so taking care of his education was the least we could do. But my family's predicament weighed heavily on his mind, and he didn't want to be a burden. He wanted to finish school as quickly as possible, so he took courses during the summer, on top of working part-time at an accounting firm. In another world, we would have liked to buy him a car or saved for a down payment to help him buy a home and get a good start on his adult life. But now we were living in a different world. And my compassionate son was more than willing to do without to benefit his extended family.

By February, Mohammad had become desperate to make a move to get his family out of Turkey. Ghouson had recovered from her miscarriage and was pregnant again. Mohammad had lost faith that my attempt to bring his family to Vancouver would ever succeed. Germany and Sweden were the two European countries that had thrown open their doors to the Syrian refugees. Those countries combined had already provided resettlement to approximately 140,000 refugees. Through the large grapevine of Syrian refugees living in Istanbul, my siblings heard that once a refugee reached Germany, the government would help their families to join them. But first you had to get there. EU countries followed a rule called the Dublin Regulation, which stated that if a refugee arrived in a foreign country from another host country that already gave refugees protection status (as was the case in Turkey), the government of the host country was obligated to either claim responsibility for that refugee or send them back to that "first country of asylum." That's one reason many EU members in Central Europe refused to open their doors to refugees: it meant taking responsibility for them.

Greece was the one exception to the rule. In 2011, the Greek government suspended the Dublin Regulation after they had problems managing asylum-seekers on a long-term basis. Most refugees simply wanted to get safe passage to Northern Europe via Greece, and so when Greece suspended the policy, refugees saw it as an opportunity to reach temporary asylum. My family heard that Greek authorities could still make life difficult for refugees who crossed its borders from Turkey. Most refugees made the journey via the Mediterranean, but some tried the land border. If refugees went by land, they had to cross the Evros River, a daunting natural border that had taken many lives, either by drowning or hypothermia. But my brothers had learned to swim in the Mighty Euphrates. So, in February 2015, Abdullah, Mohammad, and his son Shergo decided to attempt the river crossing.

They found a local who knew the road and would show them the way. They packed one small knapsack with a change of clothes, some money, and Abdullah's cellphone. Mohammad kissed his pregnant wife and his children goodbye, and the men travelled west by bus, a journey of approximately 250 kilometres. The Turkish border towns were patrolled by guards with searchlights, so they had to sneak through muddy agricultural fields to get to the river.

I found out only by accident that they were attempting that journey when I happened to call Abdullah in mid-crossing.

"What are you doing?" I asked.

"Fatima, I can't talk."

"Why are you whispering? I can barely hear you."

"We're in a field. Hiding from the police. I have to go. I'll call you when we get across the river."

I called Ghouson in a panic, and she told me about their secret plan. "We're sick and tired of this life of poverty," she said. "We don't have enough food. The kids can't go to school. We can't get to Canada, so the only choice now is Europe." Their hope was that once Mohammad, Abdullah, and Shergo got to Germany, the government would help their families join them.

Abdullah, Mohammad, and Shergo evaded detection and got to the banks of the Evros. Needless to say, it was a long day, waiting to hear back from them. All that stood between them and Greece was the raging river. They stepped into the water. It was ice-cold. Abdullah's legs immediately went numb.

"والله قلبي كان مع أولادي ومرتي, *Wallah albi kan ma'a awladi w marti.* My heart is with my wife and kids," he thought. "What will happen to Rehanna and the boys without me? I can't do that to them. I can't leave them all alone." He decided to turn back.

Mohammad and Shergo were determined to go forward. There

was an inflatable inner tube stuck in the mud on the riverbank, so they claimed it and paddled for their lives to get across the river. When they reached the riverbank on the Greek side, soaked to the bone, shaking uncontrollably, they realized that their change of clothing and money were with Abdullah. "*Yallah yallah*, come on!" they called to Abdullah. But Abdullah wouldn't cross the river.

Abdullah texted me to say that he had turned back. When I called, he said, "Oh my God, *ekhti*, sister, that river was a beast. As soon as I put my foot in it, I thought, 'Have you gone crazy?' *Inshallah*, Mohammad and Shergo make it the rest of the way."

As the sky turned dark, Mohammad and Shergo left Abdullah behind and walked west, their teeth chattering. Mohammad became feverish. He was starving, so he ate some berries from a bush. Those berries may have been poisonous, or at least rotten, because he soon began to vomit uncontrollably and became delirious, collapsing to the ground. Shergo thought his father was about to die in the middle of nowhere. As soon as he saw a human being in the distance, he called out in panic. That human being happened to be a Greek police officer. The police officer appeared to take pity on Mohammad and Shergo. He drove them to a local police station. They communicated in stunted English, and the officer nodded agreeably as he listened to their plan of attempting to get to Germany. But when they reached the station, they were put in a cell with twenty or so other shivering Syrian refugees. They were not even given a blanket. The next morning, the police guards herded the refugees into vans, the whole time promising to assist with safe passage to Germany. Instead, they were taken to the Turkish border and put back in the hands of the Turkish police. They returned to the limbo of refugee life in Istanbul. They were sick and tired, but also grateful that they had escaped death.

When I realized the risks my brothers were willing to take to get out of Turkey, I felt even more pressure to get them to Canada—fast. Once again, I bugged the UN office in Ankara. I was told that the UN might be able to issue their approval for resettlement in Canada much more quickly, but only *after* the Canadian government approved my family's asylum. So I put that G-5 application and the thick pile of required paperwork into the mail and sent it off with a prayer.

I heard nothing from the immigration office until April, when I received an email recommending I contact a sponsorship agreement holder because that path didn't require UNHCR approval. I had known that for months. It's why I had started with the SAH approach. It was so frustrating to finally hear from my government, only to be told to go back to square one. I wondered what it would take for someone in power to actually take action.

The sunshine of the early summer provided little warmth. In June 2015, I got an email from the government saying my application package was missing personal financial information from Kitt, my neighbour. She was retired and had listed her pension income, as required, but hadn't provided source documents. Kitt sent them that information right away. The very next day, the government sent another email to tell me what I already knew: since exit permits were so difficult for refugees in Turkey to attain, the Canadian government had "established a moratorium on SAHs." As an alternative to the SAH, the email continued, the government had begun a new pilot program to help privately sponsored refugees from Afghanistan, Iran, Iraq, and Syria. They were finally willing to allow *yabanci* cards in lieu of exit visas.

I couldn't believe it. I was overjoyed! Everyone in my family had *yabanci* cards. But the next paragraph smashed that joy. It stated that Syrian nationals—and only Syrian nationals—would still need the impossible-to-get documents: a *mavi kimlik* or a valid passport. A *yabanci* card would not be an acceptable alternative. Why was the Canadian government going out of its way to discriminate against Syrian refugees—the residents of the only country on the list currently going through a crisis of epic proportions? I felt as if they were taunting me. That email was not just useless for us: it was a twist of the dagger in our hearts.

By May 2016, the surge of Syrian refugees attempting to seek asylum in Europe had reached an even higher crisis point. Almost three hundred thousand refugees had applied for asylum in EU countries. That is when Mohammad set his sights once again on Germany, via the sea crossing to Kos. He said, "All my friends are getting to Germany via Kos. I'm going to Kos."

Kos was advantageous because it offered the closest proximity to Turkey's shores—a mere four kilometres from Bodrum on the Turkish coast. Mohammad was willing to risk that journey, and he could no longer wait to make his move. His family had been surviving in Turkey for three years. His teenaged kids were still working at the clothing factory, with no end in sight. His younger daughter, nine-year-old Ranim, had missed out on years of education, and his young son, seven-year-old Rezan, had never even stepped foot in a classroom. And with Ghouson pregnant, they would soon have another mouth to feed, another child facing a dismal future. They couldn't afford the smugglers' fee for the whole family, so Mohammad departed for Bodrum to make the crossing alone. He planned to reach Germany, almost two thousand kilometres away, and then he'd bring his family to him.

Mohammad didn't even tell me he was going. I found out only after he arrived in Kos. From there, he still had to take ferries to reach Athens and then cross numerous inhospitable Central European borders. But he made it safely.

That summer, more than seven million Syrians were displaced within Syria, and the number of Syrian refugees living outside their home country surpassed four million, making the Syrian crisis officially the worst refugee crisis since the Second World War. Half of those refugees were living in Turkey. In Istanbul, my family heard rumours from other Syrian refugees that the Turkish government might be planning to build a refugee camp on the Syrian side of the border, or that they might even send refugees back into Syria. Maybe those were paranoid rumours, but with all the fighting going on in Syria and along the border with Turkey, refugees were very scared; no safe harbour seemed within reach.

The refugees were victims of terrorism and global geopolitics, yet they were increasingly viewed with the same suspicion and hostility as the terrorists they had barely managed to escape. In such a climate of fear and uncertainty, more of my relatives began to talk about the possibility of fleeing to Germany via the Greek islands. After all, Mohammad had made it, and while his life at a refugee shelter was very difficult, it held the promise of a legal resettlement and a better future for his family. Some of my other cousins had also made it to Germany or Sweden.

From my remote location in Vancouver, I felt useless to my family in Syria and Turkey. To tell you the truth, I didn't feel needed at home either. By the summer of 2015, my son, Alan, was twenty-two years old; he'd grown into a smart, handsome young man. He still lived with us, but he was studying and working so hard that sometimes he didn't come home until after I had gone to bed. I guess I was feeling the early pangs of an empty nest. At such a time, some people get a pet dog or cat. I decided to get some fish. I purchased a large fish tank, put it in the space between my living room and my dining room, and bought twenty molly fish.

"*Ammeh.* Auntie, I want to see the fish," Ghalib said every time I video-chatted with them.

"Move your head, *ker*," Ghalib would nag Alan, calling his sibling the Kurdish word for donkey. Alan would respond as usual, by following his beloved older brother's every command.

I think Ghalib was a typical jealous older brother, and Alan was such a cute, happy, smiling boy that he got a lot of attention. Everywhere he went, he had this way of lighting up complete strangers. People always wanted to touch him and give him special treatment. For instance, when they went to the market to buy a kilo of rice, the vendors would beam at Alan and then say to Rehanna, "I'll give you some extra rice for that beautiful angel."

Alan was much like Abdullah as a little boy. Every time I saw that child, I wanted to reach into the screen and grab him. But it was just like admiring those fish in my tank. I couldn't hug and kiss those two boys. They might as well have been behind glass.

Abdullah did everything to take care of his family, but one thing he often neglected was himself. Abdullah's mouth remained a festering wound. He was still unable to chew most foods, and I couldn't get that picture of his mouth out of my mind. I started researching his options and contacting dentists in Turkey. I sent money for him to see a dentist. When I called the dentist to follow up, he told me it would cost about $5,000 just for dentures, and $14,000 for implants, with half the fee due up front.

Now that private sponsorships to fund my family's asylum in Canada appeared to be impossible, we could use some of that money to help Abdullah with his teeth. I talked to Rocco about it, and we agreed to finance the implants. When I told Abdullah, he didn't react the way I expected.

"Are you crazy?" he said. "Do you think I'm worth fourteen thousand dollars? I'm not worth a thousand dollars right now. And if I had that money, I would use it to feed my wife and kids. I don't care about my teeth. If I have to live this way for the rest of my life, so what? *Allah karim.*"

I convinced Abdullah to see two other dentists, but both of them gave similar estimates for the dental work. Abdullah was resolute.

"If you insist on giving me money, send me enough money to pay the smugglers to get me to Kos and then Germany. Ghalib needs to start school next year, and he needs to see a doctor for his skin: it's getting too painful for him. I want to get us to Europe. It's my best chance to help my family. Whatever happens to me in the future, we will deal with it then."

I talked to my siblings about that prospect. We had many concerns. What if he didn't survive that crossing? Or the migration to Germany? And what if he got there but he couldn't bring his family? Mohammad had tried to apply for his family's asylum, but he was shocked to find out that it could take as much as a year's time to secure approval. We started to discuss the prospect of sending enough money for Abdullah's entire family to make the crossing to Europe. I called Abdullah to ask how much it would cost to take the whole family.

"I heard the boys can go for free," he said. That meant we'd need only about $5,000.

I talked to Rocco about it, and we agreed: if that's what Abdullah wanted, that's what we would do. I called Abdullah.

"عن جد, *'an jadd?* Are you serious?" he asked.

"Do you think Rehanna and the boys could survive without you?"

"It would be so hard. And it'd be heartbreaking to have to be apart again. This way, we wouldn't have to. I'll talk to Rehanna. Call me back tomorrow."

The following day, I called. "Rehanna and I talked about it all night," he said. "When you said you'd pay for the crossing, it was like we got to the top of a mountain. We're grateful, but the things we're seeing on the news—it's scary. Rehanna doesn't know how to swim. The boys are so small. But we agreed that we will live together or we'll die together. Besides, we can't wait any longer: Rehanna is pregnant again. She doesn't feel well. She's sleeping all the time."

"*Mabrouk!* Congratulations," I said. I was happy that they had another child on the way but also worried that the journey would be too much for a pregnant Rehanna. "She needs to take vitamins and eat good food," I reminded him.

By then, I had come to better understand the difficulties my siblings had endured for years—the feeling of being stuck between a rock and a hard place. The feeling that the war would never end. That they would never be able to return home. That the world was ignoring them. Many people would crack under that kind of heartache, stress, and indifference. My family came close to breaking but did not.

I was consumed by the desire to get them to safety. I found no pleasure in my work except on payday, knowing the money would go to them. I had always loved to cook for my family and friends, but after my visit to Turkey, I found shopping depressing. The abundance of food on those shelves gave me panic attacks and filled me with a kind of bitterness that I'd never felt before. Even cooking had lost its lustre. Preparing and eating my favourite Syrian meals just made me feel the *ghorbah* more keenly, made me homesick. When I attempted to retreat to my garden trellis that had always given me a taste of Sham, it felt like such a weak substitute. Rare moments of pleasure quickly turned to guilt and shame. I did not feel grounded. My life in Canada no longer seemed to provide the best of both worlds.

At the end of every day, I would close my eyes and dream of my homeland, Damascus. I wondered, "How did my family end up in this terrible situation?" It seemed as if deep space separated us from our past lives in Syria and that, both physically and emotionally, we had drifted so far away from home that none of us would be able to return. What if I was never able to see my brothers and sisters and our *baba* again? To calm my racing thoughts, I tried to conjure up the smell of the wild jasmine in Damascus. Even for my *baba* in war-torn Sham, the air was often heavy with the smell of smoke and pulverized stone and concrete from the bombings. Now he had to worry about the new dangers that some of his children and grandchildren were about to face.

Mohammad had made that perilous crossing and reached Germany. My baby sister, Hivron, and her family were also plotting their flight to Germany via the Greek islands. Hivron had a teenaged son and three young daughters to consider; Maya, her youngest, was only eight years old. Hivron had also agreed to bring our sister Maha's second eldest son, nineteen-year-old Mahmoud. Our other sister Shireen was still in Damascus, with her husband and two younger kids, but her eldest son, Yasser, had already left Damascus and was making his way to Turkey, via Lebanon, to make the crossing with a group of his teenaged friends.

Of course, Abdullah and Rehanna still had hesitations about the plan. Aside from the many dangers of the crossing and journey to Germany, they didn't want to leave the region. They didn't want to give up their belief that the war would end soon and allow them to return to Kobani. Rehanna's *baba* Shikho was already terribly homesick for his eldest daughter and his grandsons. He was worried sick about the crossing, and the idea of their going so far away made his heart even heavier.

"It's just a temporary, emergency measure," Rehanna tried to reassure him. "The moment it's safe, we'll come back home."

With their decision made, we had one difficulty—how to get the money to Abdullah. As illegal refugees, he and Rehanna still weren't allowed to have a bank account. To get such a large amount of cash to them through friends was a big challenge. I imagined that it might take a few months of planning. But then I found that three different family friends were going to Turkey, so I asked them to each take a chunk of the money to Abdullah. With their help, I would be able to get all the money to Abdullah in just a few weeks. At the time, it seemed like a great stroke of luck.

Chapter 9

رجل قدام ورجل وراء

Rijl qiddam w rijl wara

One Foot Forward and One Backward

On July 7, Rehanna had a sharp pain in her stomach. Abdullah rushed her to the hospital. After they'd waited for hours, a nurse handed her a pill, ordered her to take it, and sent the couple home. Two days later, in the middle of the night, the pain grew worse. Rehanna started to bleed profusely. Again, Abdullah rushed her to the hospital. There she was told that she'd had a miscarriage. The doctor arranged a D & C operation—dilatation and curettage—but there weren't any anaesthetics, so Rehanna was conscious throughout the incredibly painful procedure. One of the nurses was Kurdish, and she tried to comfort Rehanna in their mother tongue. Rehanna lost a great deal of blood, and Abdullah was shocked and saddened at how weak she became and how yellow her face was after her operation.

"Tima, I so wanted to have a baby girl named Radiya, after our mother," Abdullah told me on the phone.

"نصيب, *Naseeb*. It was destiny. *Inshallah*, you will have a baby girl in the future," I said, trying to comfort him. "Take care of Rehanna. Please buy her rich food to make up her energy."

The experience steeled his resolve. Abdullah knew that he and his family had to go to Europe if they were going to secure a safe, healthy future. Rehanna was weak and anemic, but she insisted she could still make the trip. Abdullah went to the butcher and bought her iron-rich sheep livers, cans of sardines, and a large bag of dates for their journey.

July 18 was the beginning of Eid al-Fitr. Abdullah and Rehanna didn't have enough money for the typical sumptuous meal to break the Ramadan fast, but they did stick with the Muslim tradition of buying new outfits for the boys, albeit ones from the weekend flea market: jean shorts and a T-shirt for Ghalib, and for Alan, a one-piece that looked like a tuxedo shirt and pants, with a black bow tie sewn into the collar and faux suspenders. The outfit for Ghalib would be useful for their impending voyage; the one-piece for Alan was too cute to resist, and it cost only one lira at the flea market.

"*Habib albi.* Love of my heart, you look like a little man," said Abdullah, after he'd finished dressing Alan.

"How about me, Baba?" Ghalib asked.

"أنت حياتي كلها, *Inta hayati kilha.* You are my whole life."

It was a hot, sunny day, so they decided to take their stroller and walk to the Eminönü district and stroll around the Bosphorus waterfront, where passenger ferries criss-cross between the European and Asian sides of Istanbul.

"Can we take a boat ride?" Ghalib asked.

"Why not? It's Eid. It'll be fun for the boys," said Rehanna. The ferries cost one or two lira per person. The kids loved that short boat ride. Alan waved at everyone he saw. He was waving when Rehanna took a photo of Abdullah with his two boys.

Later, Abdullah would say to me, "It was like he was saying goodbye to the world."

"Is this what the boat to Europa will be like?" Ghalib wondered.

"Our boat will be a smaller version," said Abdullah, exchanging a glance with Rehanna.

After the ferry ride, they spotted a park with a kids' playground. "I was holding hands with both of the boys," recalled Abdullah. "But when they saw that playground, the boys let go and started to run. Of course, Alan tripped over his little feet and fell, but just like always, he didn't cry. I grabbed his hand, but once again, his hand slipped out of mine. He was so light and so fast, racing to the playground."

Ghalib climbed to the top of the jungle gym, but Alan was too small to do it on his own.

"Baba!" he called out, pointing to the top of the slide. So Abdullah hoisted Alan up, and followed behind, while Rehanna waited at the bottom of the slide, her cellphone's camera poised to capture the moment.

"Smile at the camera," she called out to Alan. He held up both hands and looked at his mama, who snapped the picture. Then Abdullah put Alan in his lap, and they went down the slide together, Alan laughing with delight all the way down. Abdullah texted me that picture of Alan poised at the top of the slide. He looked adorable in that little suit. But he was so pale and skinny. And his expression was so different from his typical photos. Most of the time, he was laughing or at least grinning from ear to ear. In that photo, though, he's not smiling. His big brown eyes look solemn and tentative. His hands are held up in the air, as if he's waving goodbye.

"Why is Alan so skinny?" I asked Abdullah.

"His baby teeth are coming in—the canines on the bottom. He's fussy and doesn't want to eat."

"Why don't you give him more milk?"

Abdullah sighed. "Fatima, *khallini sakit ahsan.* I'd rather be quiet than say anything."

Maybe Alan's teething was a factor. Maybe he was tired after an action-packed day. Maybe I'm reading too much into that last photograph of my beautiful nephew alive. But when I look at that picture now, I can't help but think that he looks scared.

From the moment they decided to make the crossing, Abdullah and Rehanna did their best to convince the boys that their exodus would be a wonderful adventure.

"Can we bring Pisikeh to Europa?" asked Ghalib as he pet the cat.

Rehanna laughed. "Where are we going to put it? We can bring only a small backpack."

Ghalib started to cry, until Rehanna told him that the cat had already found a lovely new home she would go to. She said, "We'll get another *pisikeh* in Europa."

"What about my bouzouki and all my toys back at home?" Ghalib wondered. Even for Ghalib, a four-year-old with no concept of the future, the trip to Europa represented a temporary fix. He still hoped and dreamed of returning to his old life in Syria.

"We'll get you a new one and new toys in Europa, and *Inshallah*, we might be back in Kobani before you even miss them."

"Do they have cookies in Europa?" Ghalib asked Abdullah.

"All kinds of delicious cookies."

"*Inshallah*, we'll have more cookies in Europa, Baba!"

Alan seconded his older brother's enthusiasm, clapping his hands and parroting the words in his baby talk language.

My friend delivered the final instalment of Abdullah's money for the smugglers at the end of July. After Abdullah texted that he had received the money, I called him.

"I'm shopping for sleeping bags," he said. It was a tip that he had gotten from other refugees who had to spend days or even weeks waiting to make the crossing and couldn't find a vacant hotel room. If that happened, they would have to camp in a park, like so many others.

The day before they departed Istanbul, Abdullah gave his two sons a bath in their inflatable pool. Next Abdullah gave his sons haircuts. Ghalib protested, so Abdullah started with Alan, who sat patiently and quietly. To convince Ghalib to sit still, Abdullah made a game of it, chasing him around the room with his buzzing clippers until the boy was exhausted enough to give in.

On August 5, Abdullah and his family left Istanbul. I was in touch with him every day. Now, when I recall those conversations and read those texts, I hear the voice of a nagging, paranoid older sister, at the whim of changing emotions, prodding her younger brother to be more cautious, to be less cautious, and ultimately, pushing him into the sea.

That first night, they reached Izmir. The port city was overrun with Syrian refugees attempting to make the crossing. At that time, the most popular departure spot was Çeşme, a coastal town on a peninsula, about an hour's drive from Izmir. From Çeşme, the Greek island of Chios was only fifteen kilometres away. But Çeşme is a windy spot—it's the kite-surfing capital of Turkey—and the weather patterns on the eastern Mediterranean are famously unpredictable there. The family went to a park where throngs of Syrian refugees congregated and camped out. Their sheer numbers made it easy for the smugglers to find their clients.

Abdullah's family rolled out their sleeping bags and collected information about their various options for exiting Turkey.

Some refugees were trying to go in shipping containers, via sea or land, but there were many stories circulating about people who had suffocated or starved to death in those containers. The majority of people placed their bets on a boat crossing to Greece from either Izmir or Bodrum to the south. But most of the refugees couldn't afford to pay smugglers for seats on big, sturdy boats, which could cost thousands of dollars per person. They had no choice but to resort to cheap, flimsy rubber dinghies, or a fishing boat, which still cost as much as $2,500 per person. Many refugees spoke of their horrific attempted crossings on dinghies.

"I have little kids. Isn't that too dangerous?" Abdullah asked the other refugees.

"We all have little kids. But we have no other choice." Everybody was in the same boat, no matter which host country they had come from: Turkey, Lebanon, Jordan, Libya. Everyone was poor and starving, their kids couldn't go to school or to the doctor. Europa was their last hope.

At that park, Abdullah started talking to smugglers. He wanted a fiberglass boat. But after a couple of days of searching and spending money on food and a hotel room, Abdullah realized their money might not last.

"We can't afford to wait around, hoping that the smugglers will find us a fiberglass boat that we can afford," Abdullah said to Rehanna.

"Maybe we should consider a rubber dinghy, like everyone else," said Rehanna. "Especially if the water is calm. If the boat is too crowded and the waves are too big, we won't go."

The next day, the family shopped for life jackets.

"*Ya haram.* It would break your heart to see so many Syrians begging on the streets, sleeping on the streets and in the parks, like paupers.

There are thousands of them here," Abdullah told me. The boys had colds, so he decided to keep their room at an inexpensive hotel.

On the morning of August 6, Abdullah texted, "It's raining hard. The smuggler said that's bad luck. He said one hundred per cent, we'll go tomorrow."

I called Abdullah to ask if they'd purchased their life jackets. Rehanna answered.

"Poor Alan. Even when I fasten the belt, I can pull the life jacket right off him," she said. We discussed tying a rope around his waist. But then the top of the life jacket might be like a cone, trapping water inside, making matters worse. I wanted to give Rehanna some comfort, so I told her that as long as she had a life jacket, she would be able to stay above water and help keep the boys afloat.

"But I don't know how to swim. I'm terrified of water. I'm like a cow."

The fact that Rehanna couldn't swim weighed heavily on Abdullah from the start. It was stressful enough that he had two young sons. But he also had to worry about Rehanna. The weather in Izmir was hot and muggy; sometimes the wind was gusty, up to eighty kilometres, and the skies were ominous, with sporadic thunderstorms. Every night for a week, they tried to leave with the smugglers. Every night, they were sent back.

August 13: "Went at 2 a.m. Police caught us and took us to their station. But they were good to us. Another family with us. They let us go this morning. Trying again tonight."

That night, there was more rain and another thunderstorm. The weather was humid, and the skies were angry. On the fourteenth and the fifteenth, I called and texted Abdullah many times. He didn't respond.

For five long days, we didn't hear from him. We were all frantic, calling and texting, waiting for any response, thinking the worst, praying for the best. Rocco and I were in Toronto visiting my in-laws. It was the longest five days of our lives. One of those nights, I had a strange dream about my mother. I dreamed that I was back home in Sham. I heard Mama yelling frantically from the living room. I rushed in to find her sitting at a computer, weeping. It was so strange to see her using a computer: when she was alive, my family didn't have a computer.

"They're talking about Abdullah on the Internet!" she yelled. "Millions of people are sending messages—so many that I think the computer is going to blow up." There was lots of crying and sadness in the messages she read, which made her worry, but she didn't know why.

"I need to get Abdullah some money," she said. She was wearing one of her favourite gold bangles, shaped like a snake. She took it off and told me to go to the jeweller and pawn it. I went to the shop, but it was packed with customers. The jeweller only had time to give the bracelet a quick look before offering somewhere between 29,000 and 31,000 lira. "Come back later, and I'll weigh it and buy it," he said. I went rushing home and told my mom the price. When I handed her the bracelet, the snake's head turned into white cloth.

That's all I can remember about that dream. While we waited for any word from Abdullah, I told my family and friends about it.

"*Inshallah kheir*," said one of my friends, an Iraqi woman. "It means someone is going to have a baby boy." I recounted the dream to my Italian mother-in-law, but she didn't know what it meant. She said she'd light a candle for the safety of my family. What none of us realized until much later was that the white cloth in the dream looked exactly like the shroud that covers a baby in traditional Muslim burials.

In the waking world, Abdullah and his family were going through their own hardships during those five days of silence. On the night of

August 13, the smuggler had called to say that he could take them on a little hard-hulled fishing boat for $4,000. The weather had cleared and the skies had gone quiet. After nightfall, the smuggler had driven them to the point at Çeşme, with six other Syrian refugees. During the hour-long ride, Ghalib and Alan were fast asleep. The smuggler told all of them to put the phone number of the local coast guard on their phones, just in case something went wrong during the crossing. Rehanna woke up Ghalib when they arrived at a rocky cove so that he could walk over it, while Abdullah carried sleeping Alan in his arms. Another smuggler was waiting in a little old fishing boat beside a rocky outcrop. The weather was warm, the sky clear, and the water calm—ideal conditions.

After they got to the beach, the smuggler revealed that the helmsman hadn't shown up. One of the Syrian refugees volunteered to steer, and the smuggler gave the man a brief tutorial on how to start the engine and operate the boat. The vessel was large enough to accommodate the eight adults. Rehanna held Alan in her lap, and Abdullah sat Ghalib on his. The huge island of Chios loomed on the horizon, the lights twinkling in the near distance. The Syrian refugee started the motor, and the smuggler pushed the boat out to sea.

"You could have walked ten times faster than that boat," said Abdullah. "We were worried that we'd get caught by the coast guard. But at least it was calm and smooth."

Within about twenty minutes, with the island of Chios just in front of them, the motor started to smoke and give off a toxic burning smell. Then it burst into flames.

"I called the smuggler and told him, 'The engine is burning!' He said, 'What am I going to do about it? Call the coast guard!' One of the refugees made that call, while the others doused the engine with sea water. *Alhamdulillah*, they were able to put out the fire. But the engine was fried. We bobbed around in that boat for what seemed like an hour and a half, but maybe it was much less time. The coast guard came and towed our boat back to a dock and made us go into the police station.

"There were about three hundred refugees at that station, all from other boats, everyone soaked and shivering and all the kids wailing. The police took down all our names. They put all of us on buses and took us to Orfa," said Abdullah, referring to the infamous Turkish refugee camp near the border with Syria, teeming with tens of thousands of refugees. That camp was close to Kobani. Rehanna was terrified that they would be returned to the region that she and the boys had fled less than a year before.

The camp at Orfa was a big, dirty warehouse suitable for storing boxes, not human beings. All the refugees were skinny and sickly, with colds and terrible coughs. The camp certainly didn't have free Wi-Fi, and Abdullah's phone had run out of data, so he couldn't contact us. This refugee "camp," like many others, was more akin to a prison: once you entered, the gates were closed and locked behind you. You were no longer allowed to move freely.

In that insect-infested camp, all that Rehanna and Abdullah could think about was how to get their boys to safety. They were granted exit only after Alan got a fever and Ghalib was bitten by some bug or insect that made his arm swollen and infected. As soon as they got out, they bought antibiotics for Ghalib and baby aspirin for Alan. Abdullah found a cafe with Wi-Fi and texted to let me know they were okay. It was August 18. I can't tell you how relieved I was to know that they were alive.

Abdullah contacted the smuggler and got his money back. Then he, Rehanna, and the boys boarded a bus, with plans to go back to Izmir. But Izmir was full of refugees, and some people told him to go to Bodrum instead, which offered a shorter sea crossing. A surge of refugees had also descended on Bodrum; more than two thousand people made that crossing in the month of August.

"It's packed here," Abdullah said when he, Rehanna, and the boys arrived in Bodrum. "Police are everywhere. Smugglers are scared. We will have to be patient and wait."

Abdullah joined the throngs of refugees who went around the city bargaining with the many smugglers during the day and waiting for the smugglers' calls at night. Abdullah, still scared to take a dinghy, told the smuggler he was hoping for a seaworthy fiberglass boat.

"Everyone has small kids, not just you. You need to pay for your boys," the smuggler said.

"But my boys are young. They will sit on our laps," Abdullah argued.

"Okay, I will let you know."

As in Izmir, the majority of refugees were sleeping in parks and on the streets because the hotels in Bodrum were booked. Ghalib and Alan still had bad colds and fevers from their days in the camp. Abdullah had to get a roof over their heads. He found another cheap hotel room, and their days of watchful waiting resumed.

"I can't go on like this," Abdullah texted me. "It's too dangerous to take a flimsy raft. The shores are so rocky they could tear apart a boat like that. Me and Rehanna are scared."

Day after day, they watched as other people made it to Greece. They hoped for good news from the smugglers about a better boat. Slowly, their money and time were running out.

"*Wallah*, we are tired of being at the hotel and waiting," Abdullah told me. "We need to finish this. If the weather's okay, I'm willing to consider a rubber dinghy. We are like everyone else here."

On August 20, Abdullah texted me. "So many police here. Waiting for the smuggler to call." I texted back with another nagging message, saying that I'd heard reports that some refugees had drowned while wearing fake life jackets. Abdullah had to reassure me that he had purchased expensive ones in Izmir for the boys and Rehanna.

The following morning, Abdullah texted again to say that they had travelled to the spot where the smugglers had another rubber dinghy at the ready. The waves were too big, and Abdullah refused to go. I am ashamed to admit this now, but by then, I had started to become impatient. The suspense, the anxiety, the fear, and the doubt were driving me crazy. I called Abdullah.

"What are you waiting for? What's wrong with you, Abdullah?" I demanded.

"Fatima, you don't understand. The waves were too big last night. There were fifty refugees for one flimsy dinghy. I'm not putting my babies in a situation like that."

"Everybody else is taking the risk. Our friends and relatives told me many refugees make it there safely," I had the nerve to respond.

"Sister, stop pushing me. Do you think we're happy here? والله تعبنا, *Wallah ta'abna.* We're sick and tired."

"How much do you have now?"

"A little more than four thousand dollars."

"Tell them you have only four thousand and you have babies."

"أختي، بيعرفوا، ما بيهمّن, *Ekhti biya'arfo, ma beyhemmon.* Sister, they know that. They don't care."

"Talk to other refugees and smugglers. You need to find your way."

On August 22, I called Abdullah again with a different concern. There were media reports that in Central Europe authorities refused to let the surge of refugees pass through; some were robbed and beaten. Even in Greece, the situation seemed grim.

"I don't think you should go to Europe. I think you should go back to Istanbul," I said.

"One minute you're pushing me to go and the next you're pushing me to stay put," Abdullah responded. "أختي خلص، ما في رجعة, *Ekhti khalas mafi raga'a.* Sister, enough! There's no going back."

Throughout that month, the clock was ticking louder in my brother's ear. Every day, he was chipping away at their four-thousand-dollar fund. Every day, he had to face the possibility that they would have to travel on an overcrowded rubber dinghy. Every day, he was reminded that Mohammad was already in Germany, and so were at least four of our cousins, while other relatives were at that very moment attempting to traverse the northern land corridor into Germany. Hivron and her family were poised to make the crossing, and so was Shireen's son Yasser. Of course, none of those people had two tiny kids and a frightened wife to safeguard.

On August 23, I woke up before the dawn, as usual: no texts from Abdullah.

"Where are you? What's going on?" my text demanded.

"On the street. The waves were too big last night. I just saw Yasser. He'll tell you the waves were too big. It's too windy here."

I'm ashamed to admit my response. "Everyone is going except for you, why are you scared?"

"I can't explain it. When you're in the water, it's so different than it is from afar. It's like a horror movie."

On the night of August 23, the water and the wind had made peace with each other, or at least that's how it appeared from Bodrum. Abdullah waited all night for the smugglers' call, until the sun rose once again over a tranquil sea and another day of watchful waiting began.

On August 25, I woke up before the sun to find that Abdullah had sent me a video of the waves and the wind from a few nights before, asking, "Would you get into that sea? Do you understand?" That video chilled me to the bone. It gave me some appreciation of the refugees' terrifying situation. When I think about it now, I feel like an idiot for pushing. On Google Maps, Bodrum looks like the ideal place to cross from. But the point at Akyarlar juts out from the coastline, and because of that, it's often windy there. The winds can be so bad that they have a famous name among mariners: the Meltemi winds. They peak in the summer until mid-September. Conditions before a Meltemi are often ideal: skies are blue and the wind is typically lighter, making it seem like a perfect time for a boat ride. But the winds can rear up suddenly, particularly around Bodrum and Kos, reaching gale-force speeds of more than thirty knots, generating steep waves of three to six metres.

The Meltemi winds didn't cause all the drownings that were happening across the Mediterranean, but they certainly helped provide the perfect storm. If I had done more research in advance, I don't know if I would have sponsored Abdullah's crossing. Or maybe I would have sent more money to pay for a seaworthy boat—two more what-ifs that I will never be able to change.

By the time Abdullah texted the next day to say, "We're going tonight," I had become skeptical that a crossing would happen. Maybe he was too. Since that first night of sleeping in the park in Izmir, the family had been staying in one hotel room after the other, checking out each day in the hopes that they would cross that night, only to be returned to the shore to search for a new hotel room in two cities overwhelmed with refugees looking for cheap hotel rooms. That day, Abdullah had finally found a decent, affordable room, and he decided that they wouldn't check out before they made each and every crossing attempt. Instead, he paid the hotel owner the day's fee, so that if the overnight crossing attempt was unsuccessful, the family could immediately return to their room.

That afternoon of August 26, before they left to make the crossing, Abdullah bought some supplies: a few bottles of water for the voyage and some hard cookies to soothe Alan's teething and Ghalib's cookie cravings. At midnight, they left the hotel, carrying the sleeping boys in their arms. They walked for about five minutes to the rendezvous point and piled into a passenger van with at least a dozen refugees, a mix of single adults and families with kids. The smuggler warned everyone to be silent when they got to the beach.

"If any of your babies cry, we'll get caught."

The van drove for at least a half-hour. They arrived at the cove, and when they got to the shore, there were more than forty refugees waiting—all designated for a rubber dinghy with a capacity of no more than twenty. The wind was strong and the dinghy was a weak match for the waves. It groaned under the weight of the refugees as they clambered on. Abdullah and Rehanna stood on the shore. They didn't know whether to get in that dinghy or turn back. Soon they were the only refugees left on the shore.

"رجل قدام ورجل وراء, *Rijl qiddam w rijl wara*. One foot forward and one backward," thought Abdullah.

"You need to leave right now! Get on the boat," hissed the smuggler.

"There are too many people here. You didn't say there would be so many of us. It's too dangerous," Abdullah countered.

"*Yallah, yallah*. Come on, hurry! We have to go!" the other refugees called out. "Either we live together or we die together. We all suffer the same."

Rehanna grabbed Abdullah's hand and squeezed, saying, "*Inshallah, we'll make it.*"

Abdullah paid the smuggler, and they waded into the shallows, carrying the boys. Abdullah got in the dinghy first and Rehanna lifted the boys up to him one by one. Once on board, they squeezed into a spot in the middle among the other parents with kids. Abdullah had Ghalib in his lap and Rehanna had Alan; they hugged the kids to their chests, with their arms around them like seat belts.

"*Ya haram*, that dinghy was so packed," Abdullah told me, "we could barely breathe. But we were desperate. No one on the outside can understand what it was like for us. They'd wonder, 'Why would they put their kids in danger like that?' When I looked the other refugees in the eye, everyone had the same grim look of determination. All their eyes could see was Europa; it was like they were looking at heaven. Everyone was praying, '*Inshallah*, the coast guard will be blind to us. *Inshallah*, we'll survive and get to Greece.' "

The boat sped toward the open water. With every inch they crossed, the waves grew higher and higher, the wind stronger, stirring the sea up into a rabid froth. The sparkling lights of Kos seemed even more remote.

"Each wave would take the front of the dinghy up, up, up, until we thought that it would flip over," Abdullah told me later. "But then it would crest the wave and plunge downward, so that the back of the boat would shoot up into the sky."

The centre of the dinghy, where the families were sitting, started to fill with water. Ghalib was scared and crying, as was Rehanna. Abdullah was scared too, but amazingly, Alan was quiet. Everyone started to bail the water out from the middle of the dinghy with their hands.

"How stupid are we to do this to our kids, to ourselves?" Abdullah asked Rehanna. "How did we end up in this nightmare? All these refugees escaped the war and now we're in this flimsy boat?"

"I know, but we can't go back," Rehanna said.

It went on like that for what seemed like an hour. But when you're panicking, time plays tricks on you. It might have been ten minutes or so. Then the seas got worse.

"The waves were getting higher," Abdullah said. "The farther into the sea we went, the more dangerous it got. Our hearts were beating so fast and we thought, 'There's no way we'll live through this.' Everyone was praying for the coast guard to be blind to our boat, but Rehanna and I were praying to God that they would see it and save us, because otherwise we would not survive those waves. Then, *Alhamdulillah*, suddenly a boat appeared, flashing a searchlight across the water. The spotlight landed on our dinghy and that boat sped toward us. We were so relieved.

"But the men on board the approaching boat were yelling angrily at us. They threw a big rope, and it whacked the dinghy driver hard in the head. They had what looked like a big spear, but maybe it was a hook, to pull the boat closer. Whatever it was, they were poking the boat with it. Everyone on the boat was hysterical, yelling, 'منشان الله, *Minshan Allah!* For God's sake, don't rip our boat! حرام عليكم, *Haram 'alaikom.* We have little kids!' Some people wanted to grab hold of the rope so they could be towed back to land, but others wanted to get away so they could continue with the crossing. Many people jumped up at once, tipping the boat. A few people fell into the sea, but luckily, the refugees pulled those people back into the dinghy. The whole time, those waves were crashing against us. It was chaos. The refugees finally grabbed hold of the rope and we were towed back to Turkey."

When they reached the dock, the authorities simply waved a finger at the refugees, saying, "Don't try that again." Then they were sent on their way.

Abdullah and Rehanna carried their exhausted boys back to the hotel, where they laid out their clothes to dry and slept until the afternoon. The next day, Abdullah went for a walk with Ghalib, and then he returned to the smuggler to get his money back. After their ordeal, Abdullah and Rehanna needed a few days to recover and think about what they would do next.

Their hotel had one great luxury: a pool where the boys could have some fun and where Abdullah might be able to make them more comfortable in the water. Alan loved paddling around in that pool. But Ghalib had never liked the water, and the attempted crossing had petrified him even more. Maybe the chlorine also stung his rash, which had become angrier during the days in that Izmir camp.

Abdullah and Rehanna decided to try the sea crossing again. Now I had a new concern on my mind. I was worried that if Abdullah lost his cellphone during the crossing, he wouldn't be able to call us and let us know he was okay. I called Rehanna and asked her to write down all our phone numbers on a slip of paper and put that piece of paper in something plastic and watertight, just in case. I could hear the boys in the background, playing; Alan, as usual, was laughing.

My final text from Abdullah came on August 31. It was seven p.m. for me, and in Turkey it was the morning of September 1. The text read, "God willing, we're leaving tonight."

That morning, Abdullah met with the smuggler again.

"Please, my kids will not survive in a rubber dinghy. I need a hard-backed boat. Can't you give me a discount?"

"Can you pay more?" asked the smuggler.

"I only have four thousand dollars. I can't get a penny more."

"Then you'll have to settle for a rubber dinghy," said the smuggler.

"I'm not risking another rubber dinghy," said Abdullah, and he walked away with a heavy heart. He returned to the hotel room and broke the news to Rehanna. They didn't know what to do. Time was their enemy. If they stayed even one more night, they might not even have enough money for a dinghy.

A few hours later, the smuggler called and said, "I will agree to the four thousand for a hard boat. But you have to make sure that your boys don't make a sound. If they so much as breathe heavily, I will call it off."

"Don't worry. Thank you," Abdullah said.

Abdullah and Rehanna once again prepared for the crossing. Rehanna had the list of our phone numbers wrapped in plastic. When Abdullah placed the list in his pocket, he found some Turkish coins. What would he need those coins for in Greece? He put them on the dresser.

Ghalib noticed and said, "What are you doing, Baba? That's a lot of money. I want to keep those coins." Abdullah put the coins back in his pocket with the phone numbers.

Rehanna and Abdullah dressed the boys for the journey. Ghalib wore blue shorts and a blue shirt. Alan wore the red T-shirt and long blue jean shorts that I had purchased for him in Turkey. Both boys lay down for a nap and were soon fast asleep.

The sun set and the sky turned dark. It was a warm night. Ghalib woke up hungry. They were feeling stir-crazy after so many nights of doing the same thing, so they decided to get something to eat, then go to a park near the rendezvous point and wait for the smuggler's call. Abdullah put Alan's shoes on, securing the Velcro straps and then kissing them, over and over. "Alan was still half asleep, but he smiled," said Abdullah recently. "يا ربي قد ايش بست هالبوط, *Ya rabbi, addeish biset halboot.* Oh God, how many times I kissed those shoes."

"Stop it or you'll wake him up," Rehanna told Abdullah.

Abdullah gathered Alan's warm, sleeping body in his arms and they left the hotel.

"I bought one Turkish bun. I gave it to Rehanna and told her to take half and split the other half for Alan and Ghalib."

Abdullah and Rehanna were anxious. They didn't want any surprises, so Abdullah called the smuggler and demanded to see the boat in advance. The smuggler agreed. He met Abdullah near the park, and they drove for more than an hour, heading west and around the point at Akyarlar, then north along a road that hugged the shore. That area was very busy with tourists and hotels and lively restaurants and bars. They passed a few strips of beach and finally arrived at a spot near a marina.

"We went down to the water. There was a tiny fiberglass boat and a Turkish man," Abdullah said. "The owner, the Turkish man, was scratching something off the hull of the boat—probably the boat's name. The boat looked okay, but it was small: big enough for six adults at most. The smuggler assured me that there were only a few more passengers. The Turkish guy and the Syrian were whispering to each other in Turkish."

"He's worried about your kids," said the Syrian smuggler. "This is a busy, sensitive area. Even a whisper will echo on the water. If your kids cry, we will get caught."

Abdullah promised that the boys would be quiet. Then he handed over his fee.

"Be ready for my call," said the smuggler, as he dropped Abdullah off near the park.

"I paid the money. We are leaving in an hour or so," Abdullah said to Rehanna when they met back at the park.

"توكلنا على الله, *Tawakkalna ala Allah*. Trust in Allah's plan. We need to finish this," Rehanna said.

Alan was still sleeping, but Ghalib was awake.

"حبيبي راح نروح على أوروبا, *Habibi*, we're going to Europa, say *Inshallah*," Abdullah said. "But we'll need to be very quiet when we get to the boat. We can't talk at all until we get to Europa. And when we get to Europa, I'll get you lots and lots of cookies."

The temperature was perfect—twenty-one degrees—the humidity was low, and the wind was light. When the sky turned dark, it was filled with stars, and the moon was only starting to wane. I imagine Rehanna pointing up to the sky and marveling at that moon and those stars with her typical optimism. But I've never had the heart to ask Abdullah if what I see in my mind is accurate.

The smuggler's call came a little after midnight. Abdullah and Rehanna carried their sleeping boys to the rendezvous point nearby. Soon after, a car pulled up. Aside from the smuggler, there were two male refugees in the front seat, and a woman and young girl in the back. Abdullah and Rehanna got into the back with the boys in their laps.

During the hour-long drive, Alan and Ghalib were fast asleep. The touristy areas were quieter, but the bars and streets around the marina were still quite busy. As they got out of the car and the smuggler guided the group toward the boat, another family appeared—a husband, wife, and three children. It now seemed that there were too many people for the boat. Abdullah and Rehanna didn't know what to do. Financially, could they afford to hold out for another fiberglass boat or even another rubber dinghy, even for a few more days? Could they afford to give up on Europe and return to Istanbul? The kids were already so skinny and sickly: would they survive another winter? There was already a hint of autumn cool in that late summer wind. Abdullah couldn't have known that the choice he was about to make would change his life and also change the world.

Chapter 10

الله يرحمن

Allah yerhamon

God Rest Them in Peace

From the time I received Abdullah's first text from Izmir to the time I got his final text on the night of August 31, I called Baba every night. "ربي يسر ولا تعسر", *Rabbi yassir wa la tu'assir.* Oh God, please ease their troubles," he would say.

I waited for Abdullah's texts, or any news from my family, anything to indicate that they were still alive. In those many hours between texts and conversations, my mind raced back and forth, from the sunny spots to its darkest corners, thinking the worst, hoping for the best, searching for clues that I might have missed within our chain of text messages, monitoring any news I could find, watching the video Abdullah had sent of the waves. Our whole family was praying for them to cross safely.

Since early August, I had been living in two worlds. In one world, I was a wife and mother and hairdresser living a lovely life in Vancouver, Canada. In the other world, I was helping my family, desperate Syrian refugees who had given up hope of a sustainable life in Istanbul and had turned their sights on Kos. These two worlds were separated by ten thousand kilometres and eight time zones. If you asked my husband and my son which of those worlds I spent the most time in, they would have said the latter.

On August 28, I read the horrifying news that a refrigerator truck was found in Austria containing the bodies of seventy-one refugees, four of them children. In Macedonia, Bulgaria, and Hungary, the governments had chosen to deal with the surge of refugees by building higher fences to keep them out. But none of these stories seemed to grab the public's attention. Perhaps the news was too terrible and depressing to imagine, so people who did hear about it simply blocked it out. I can't blame them. I used to be like that once too.

On September 1, I woke up long before the sun rose. I sent Abdullah many messages, nagging him to text me back. I was glued to my cellphone all day, checking it compulsively.

I called Baba. "Did you hear anything from Abdullah?"

"لا، إن شاء الله خير, *La, Inshallah kheir.* No, but God willing everything will be all right."

"He told me that the journey would only take thirty minutes!" I said.

"Maybe he didn't leave yet, or he ran out of minutes on his phone so he can't call us," Baba said, trying to calm me down. "You know how it's been for them the last month."

I hoped Baba was right, but nothing could calm my fears. I called my sisters and we worried together. "قلبي عم يغلي. My heart is boiling," we would say to each other.

As night fell in Vancouver, I was stressed and tired. I put my phone on the kitchen table and went to bed early, as usual. Afterward, I was racked with guilt for the simple fact that I had gone to sleep. I woke up at about five a.m., my heart banging against my chest. In Turkey, it was already afternoon. I raced to the kitchen and found I'd received dozens of missed calls—from Shireen, Maha, Hivron, Ghouson, and my father.

Why were they all calling me at the same time? I was shaking, and I could feel my pulse racing. I phoned Shireen in Damascus, and she answered right away, but the signal was bad.

Shireen was crying and screaming. All I could hear was her repeating Abdullah's name.

"شو بيه عبدالله, *Sho beeh, Abdullah?* What's wrong with Abdullah?" I yelled.

I let out a loud scream and started to cry. "ياالله في شي. Oh God, something's wrong!" I yelled. It woke my husband and son, and they came rushing into the kitchen.

"Something happened to Abdullah," I said. I was crying so loud that they couldn't understand what I was saying.

"Find me Ghouson's number," I said to Rocco. My hands were shaking so badly, I couldn't hold the phone. When I reached Ghouson, she sounded like she'd been crying.

"Why are you crying?" I asked.

"ولاد عبدالله وريحانة ماتوا, *Wlad Abdullah w Rehanna mato.* Abdullah's kids and Rehanna died," she wailed.

"*Sho? Keef? Aimteh?* What? How? When? Where's Abdullah?"

"He's in the hospital. Standing in front of three dead bodies."

I dropped the phone and started to scream. I collapsed on the floor. I slapped my face and pulled at my hair. I wanted to hurt myself.

"*Ya Allah, laysh? Ya Allah, la la.* Oh God, why? No, no! كله مني‎, *Kolo minni.* It's all my fault!"

If I hadn't sent the money for the smugglers, Rehanna, Ghalib, and Alan would still be alive. If I hadn't become obsessed with Abdullah's teeth and offered to pay for implants, he would never have asked me for such a large sum of money to take that crossing to Kos instead. If I had been more generous with money when they were living in Istanbul—for food, for rent, for milk, for Ghalib's eczema medication—maybe they wouldn't have had to resort to attempting that crossing. Too many what ifs, crashing into each other.

Rocco picked me up and put his arms around me. But it made me feel like a cornered animal. I squirmed out of his grip and began to shriek "Why?" over and over again. Rocco and Alan sat me down on the living room couch. I wailed even louder. I wanted to scream so loud the world would hear me. When I closed my eyes, all I could see were those boys' faces. All those calls, all those videos and photographs my brother had so proudly sent me of his boys. At that moment, their voices and their laughter rang in my ears. I could not believe that those voices had suddenly gone silent. I felt as if Abdullah was dead too. His family was his whole life. He had lost everything that mattered. Now, without them, how would he go on? And who would he become?

I have to think hard to be able to recall what happened after that. It's like trying to make sense of a nightmare. I collected many pieces of this story after the fact, because I was too consumed by grief to care about details in the moment. I talked at length to Abdullah and my family; I read and re-read news and social media reports; I reviewed my text messages and emails.

In many ways, I was just like you, an outsider looking in, trying to understand the tragedy and the flood of information. I remember calling my sisters. Most of the time, we didn't speak. We just cried together. When I called home to talk to Baba, Shireen answered his phone.

"I'm worried about Baba's heart," she whispered. "He can't even stand; his legs won't hold him up. He's been sitting on the floor for hours. Sometimes he's weeping and sometimes he's just completely silent. He wants to go to Kobani for the burial. But that's crazy. We said, '*Allah yerhamon*. God rest them in peace. You can't get there in time for the funeral. And it's too dangerous anyway.'"

Shireen handed the phone to Baba. We had no words except for "*Allah yerhamon.*"

I was desperate to hear Abdullah's voice. But we couldn't call him; his cellphone was in the sea. I knew only that Abdullah arrived at the hospital in Bodrum early that morning and was confronted with the bodies of his wife and children. He knew he had to call his family and deliver the terrible news. He remembered that plastic-wrapped slip of paper containing our phone numbers. When he reached into his pocket and found the Turkish coins that Ghalib had begged him to keep, he started to weep. A stranger saw Abdullah crying over those coins. He handed Abdullah his cellphone to call our relatives. That beautiful man said, "Take the phone. It's yours to keep."

The first person Abdullah reached was Ghouson. He asked her to share the grim news with the rest of the family. By nine a.m., a few close friends had arrived at our home to be by my side. It was already seven p.m. in Turkey. I asked Rocco, "Please go on the Internet and see if anyone is talking about what happened to their boat."

When he came back with the iPad, he looked like he had seen a ghost.

"My sister, Anna, just sent something to me. I don't know if you should see this."

I grabbed the iPad from his hands. That's when I saw the photograph of Alan for the first time. The shot of that little boy, Abdullah's son, my nephew, face down on the beach in a red T-shirt and blue jean shorts—the clothes I had bought for him in 2014 during my visit to Istanbul, the clothes I had touched with my own hands.

"This is Alan," I cried.

"Are you sure?" Rocco asked me.

"I think so."

I texted the picture to Ghouson, but she didn't reply. I phoned her and she was crying.

"هاد آلان, *Had Alan*. It's Alan," she sobbed. "He was wearing those clothes when they left Istanbul."

To this day, it makes me sick to think about that photograph of Alan, even though I carry it with me everywhere I go. It is burned into my mind and tattooed onto my heart. It's impossible to describe exactly how it struck me in that first moment. Maybe it's not even necessary to do so. It probably struck you in a similar way. It conveys two things at once. On the one hand, it's the familiar and tender pose of a toddler sleeping, his body awkwardly contorted, yet he's sound asleep nonetheless, his fat little cheek pressed against the mattress. But it's not a mattress. It's wet, cold sand. And he's not asleep. He is dead. Everything about the setting is so very wrong. He's at the edge of the tide line. The water is lapping against his face. You are simultaneously overtaken by panic and urgency—a need to act quickly to remove him from harm's way before it's too late. Then you realize, it's already too late. You cannot save him. I could not save him. All at once, that photograph conveys our greatest joys and our darkest fears. Whether you are a parent or an auntie like me, a teenager or an elder, you feel as though you have stumbled upon a terrible accident. This has happened to someone too young and vulnerable to properly care for himself. A boy who died under your watch.

Of course, to us, the blood relatives of Alan, that photograph cut so much deeper. Because family is supposed to provide the first line of defense and protection. Family is supposed to keep their young safe. Even though we knew that Alan was dead, that photograph made it an unavoidable fact. We had not been there for him in the most desperate, and certainly the most terrifying, minutes of his life.

I will never be able to understand what that tragedy did to my brother Abdullah. I will never be able to understand how much that photograph of Alan devastated an already traumatized father. For me, it was proof not just that all my attempts to help safeguard Rehanna, Ghalib, and Alan's lives had been useless. It was proof that I had provided the wind that drove them into that sea.

The photograph of Alan went viral on social media soon after the Turkish photographer posted it on Twitter. The news outlets picked up the image and ran with it. Before noon, Vancouver time, the British and European media had already published the image of "the boy on the beach." The North American media followed suit. Many of them didn't even know his name. All the media outlets eventually provided a name, but it was the wrong one: Aylan, based on a misspelling by the Turkish authorities. Ghalib's name was also misspelled, as Galip.

For my family, that initial media coverage made the wound even deeper. Isn't it reckless to publish a picture of a dead child before knowing if the boy's family members have been notified? My sister Shireen's son Yasser had reached Kos just two days prior to the tragedy. We knew that he had made it out of Greece and was somewhere in Central Europe. But that terrible morning, Shireen didn't know of his exact whereabouts. Imagine how she felt, waiting for word from her son and hoping that he didn't see the photograph of his cousin or read any newspapers before she was able to break the news to him.

"Breaking news" is an apt term for the way that photograph smashed my family into pieces. When I tried to read those initial media reports, anger pierced through my grief. I wanted to set the record straight and give back my nephews' names and dignity. And I wanted the world to understand how and why they had drowned, washed up on a beach, a thousand kilometres from their homeland. But first, I needed to talk to Abdullah. Finally, at five p.m. my time, I got to speak to him. It was after midnight for him. He had been to the morgue and his mind was haunted by the sight of his wife and sons' dead bodies, which he had seen at least twice, first to identify them, then later, after they had been autopsied.

"Their chests are all stitched up. That would hurt so much," he said, as if they had still been alive during the autopsies and could feel the pain of the scalpel.

"Ghalib is covered with scratches and bruises." Perhaps from hitting all those rocks along the shore, where his and Rehanna's bodies were found.

"You should see my Rehanna now," he wailed. "She looks like a balloon. Her body is so bloated, like she drank the sea. Why?"

"It's all my fault," I wailed.

"No, Fatima, you are the best sister in the world. You always did your best for me, for our family. هاد قدر من الله, *Hada qadar min Allah*. It's the fate of God." Even in his darkest hours, in the dark of night, my brother tried to comfort me.

For a few minutes, we had no words and communicated with our sobs.

"*Habibi, sho saar?* Sweetheart, tell me what happened on the boat."

"The waves were so high, the boat capsized. I did everything I could to save them, but I have only two hands. I was trying to hold Rehanna with one hand and the boys with another. Then Rehanna said, '*Enkez alawlad.* Save the kids.' It's the last thing she said to me. *Allah yerhamha.* God rest her in peace. I tried to save them, but the waves were crashing. One by one, they slipped from my hands."

We cried again. Then I told Abdullah about the photo of Alan, saying it was all over the news and social media.

"I can't look at it, I can't," he said, and lapsed back into tears. Eventually he said, "*Inshallah,* it will be the wake-up call to the world, so it will help others. People have been dying for far too long. People need to see the reality of all the suffering refugees. My boys had such a short life. Why did this happen to them?"

I could think of no answer that would provide solace. He was still in shock from the trauma of that terrible night at sea and its aftermath.

"I always came home from work with a banana for the boys," he sobbed. "موزة واحدة, *Mozeh wahdeh,* just one banana, that I would split in half. I didn't have enough money to buy two. The boys loved bananas. I should have bought one for each of them. I will put a banana on each of their graves."

"والله حرام, *Wallah haram.* This has to be a message from God," he said. "That he wants us to love and have peace and be human beings. الله حط النور على آلان, *Allah hatt alnoor 'ala Alan,* God shone the light on Alan, منشان يصحي العالم, *Minshan yissahi al-'alam.* This picture is a wake-up call to the world. This war needs to stop. We need to stop people from drowning."

After another long silence, Abdullah talked some more. "After I left the morgue, I went back to the beach. There was a refugee family with small children, carrying life jackets. Sister, I begged them, 'Please don't go. You're alive. Who cares if you're hungry? You are alive.' But they barely noticed me. As the mother passed by, I kept begging her to turn back. She looked at me and said, 'We're already dead.'"

He told me that he had to get off the phone because the media wanted to talk to him. When the line went dead, I was once again struck by the feeling that he was dead too, that I would never see him again. His words rang in my head over and over again: "They had such a short life." And, "This picture is a wake-up call to the world."

That's when I got off the couch. I needed to add my voice to Alan's. I needed to share their true names and their true stories with the world to keep their voices alive. I was just a hairdresser living on the opposite side of the world from Syria. I had no connections to powerful people. All my attempts to provide a safe haven for my family had failed. But I had a luxury that my family didn't: I spoke English. Maybe I could become the translator for my family and for so many millions of suffering Syrians who had no voice. Maybe I could keep the spotlight shining and prevent all these people from falling back to sleep. But I was still in shock. I didn't know how to make myself heard. I asked Rocco to email the CBC's *Go Public* news program and forward the photo of Alan to them, and also to talk to our MP, Fin Donnelly. If I slept at all that first night, I did not know it. In the middle of the night, I put a post on Facebook with a photo of Alan and Ghalib laughing. I wanted the world to see them as living, breathing, laughing young boys.

The next morning, a dozen reporters and camera operators appeared in my front yard. I must have brushed my hair and washed my face and changed my clothes, but I have no memory of doing such things. I went outside and sat in a chair that Rocco or Alan or one of my friends had placed there. Two framed photographs of Ghalib and Alan were placed beside me, and my family and friends stood behind me as I faced the cameras and microphones.

I began to talk. I could not even attempt to hold back my tears. I just cried and talked, as if I were confessing my crimes to a jury of my peers. I repeated what Abdullah had told me about what happened at sea. I blamed myself for sending him the money for the smugglers. I said that I had applied for asylum in Canada for Mohammad's family and that I had begun the process for Abdullah's family too, but my application for Mohammad had been rejected.

Time or a chronology of events was entirely missing from my monologue. As thoughts popped into my head, I repeated them. I said that I had been to Turkey the previous year and I had seen for myself the hardships of Syrian refugees. I mentioned something about my desire to get Abdullah treatment for his teeth, mumbling that this was "another story." I confessed that I should have done more to support my family. I regretted not buying my nephews more toys. I recalled a conversation with Ghalib before they left Istanbul. He had asked me for a bicycle, and I had promised my nephew I would send him money for that.

When I stopped talking, a reporter asked if I blamed the Canadian government for their deaths. I said I blamed the whole world for turning its back on the Syrian people. I said I was there to deliver my brother's plea to the public, to find any way to prevent more tragic deaths, and to stop the war in Syria.

When it was over, I literally stumbled up the stairs leading to my front door.

Over the next forty-eight hours, my family, like everyone else, had to rely on Internet reports for more information. And with the public clamouring for more background, more specific details, many news outlets carried different, confusing, sometimes contradictory reports. The world wanted to know everything about the little boy on the beach before they even knew his name.

On September 3, the world learned the correct name of the boy on the beach and the names of his loved ones. I had provided the correct spelling of both boys' names during my press conference. Some reports skewed my words, saying that I claimed that I had applied for asylum for Abdullah's family, even though I repeated twice that I had sent the government only an application for Mohammad's family.

Another thing that haunts me to this day is that during the press conference, I myself miscommunicated something Abdullah had told me during our many conversations. When he told me that Rehanna looked bloated, like a balloon, I assumed that he was referring to the way she looked right after she drowned. But that's the way she looked much later, when he identified her body at the hospital. When I spoke to the media, I was still grieving, so my mind couldn't hold on to much, and what little I could remember was filtered through grief. I tried to correct the facts later, but people had latched on to the misinformation from my own mouth.

I was shocked that even in the immediate aftermath of the tragedy, a segment of the population was looking hard for information that might discredit my brother, and they latched on to my words, using them to spread hate and racism. In the West, we call those people trolls. Whatever name you give them, they cast a long, ugly shadow upon an already grim time for me and my family.

With the media and the public hungry for information, I tried to sort through everything that was reported. Luckily, I had Alan and Rocco to monitor the news and social media. I received many emails and messages from people all over the world who wanted to help my family, but I did not have the strength to communicate with anyone. The daily onslaught of gossip did not penetrate my bubble of grief and my desperate longing to be with my family. The Arabic media and the Arabic public placed a lot of significance on the way Alan's body was lying on that shore, with his shoes in the foreground. People in the Middle East think that it's a bad sign to see the soles of someone's shoes, and therefore many people believed that his pose conveyed the message that Alan was upset, casting shame on a callous and hostile world.

This detail mattered to Abdullah most of all. He had kissed those shoes many times before leaving the hotel that night. Now that he had lost his wife and sons, he was also losing himself. Slowly, I began to filter out the noise and piece together the media's version of what happened. During the early morning hours of September 2, Alan's body washed ashore on Golden Beach in Akyarlar, Turkey. Rehanna and Ghalib were discovered a little later on the nearby rocky shores, about a hundred metres away from Alan's body. The photographer had also taken photos and videos of Ghalib, lying on his back, his T-shirt pulled up to reveal his belly and chest. He looked like he was sleeping too.

A bartender who worked at a restaurant on Golden Beach claimed that he arrived at work at six thirty a.m. and saw two bodies floating in the water: one was Alan and the other a little girl wearing pink jeans. He told reporters that he dashed into the water to pull them onto the sand; when it appeared they were dead, he said he closed their eyes and called an ambulance. There was no mention that he tried to take Alan's pulse or perform CPR.

And yet, why was Alan's body still at the edge of the shore when the Turkish photographer appeared? Perhaps the bartender meant to comfort our family. But we weren't comforted, only more bewildered and stunned. How could a tiny boy's body be left at the edge of the shore?

And then there was the matter of how the photographs of the boy on the beach came to be. According to the Turkish photographer who took those pictures, she was out on that beach at six a.m., taking photographs of a group of Pakistani refugees attempting to make the boat crossing to Greece. That's when she came across Alan, Ghalib, and the little girl wearing pink jeans. She took many pictures of Alan, including some that feature a Turkish police officer towering over Alan's body as he talks with another police officer. One Turkish police officer carried Alan to a rocky area, placing his body behind a big rock, perhaps to hide him from the tourists, while someone shot footage of the officer doing this. Can you imagine how my brother felt when he watched that video? To see his younger son treated like refuse?

The photographer sent those photos to her newspaper, Dogan News Agency. They published the picture of Alan that same morning, along with an article about the tragedy. The photographer also posted the picture of Alan on Twitter with the hashtag #KiyiyaVuranInsanlik, which means "humanity washed ashore."

Throughout those first few days, my son Alan witnessed the spread of the photo on social media. But we didn't know the extent of its reach until many months later. A group of university researchers conducted a study about it. Within twelve hours, the photo had reached 20 million screens. A handful of initial tweets by refugee advocates and journalists quickly led to fifty-three thousand tweets per hour. The viral tweet also changed the entire tone of the public conversation about refugees. Until that day, people commonly used the term *migrant*, as if refugees fleeing war had a choice to migrate. After September 2, people started using the term *refugee* much more often.

But what happened on that beach early that morning? Was the bartender the first person to discover and move Alan's body? When did the photojournalist capture the police officer removing Alan's body from the shore? How many people touched his body? And for what purpose? And what of Rehanna's and Ghalib's bodies? What about the girl in the pink jeans? Didn't they deserve some vigilance and decency too?

My family had to make do with the same pictures and videos and articles that the rest of the world was receiving. The eyes of the cameras became our eyes on Abdullah's lost world. I watched footage of Abdullah as he exited the morgue, his face crumpled in grief, the cameras unrelenting as he turned his face to the wall and sobbed. He tried to describe what it's like to lose your whole world to a bunch of foreign journalists speaking Turkish and English and other languages he did not know. And if his words got lost in translation, how would he know?

When I spoke with Abdullah the next day, he was in a hysterical state. At the hospital, he had been given a bag containing his family's clothes and shoes.

"It shattered my heart to have to take that bag of clothes, knowing it's the only thing that's left of them," Abdullah cried. "My hands were shaking. I couldn't even carry it."

"الله يصبرك, *Allah yissbrak*. God give you patience," I said. I wanted to fly there to be with Abdullah, but Ghouson called to say that some of our relatives would be with him soon. For the time being, though, it was painful to know that my brother was suffering alone. After leaving the hospital, Abdullah returned to the hotel where he, Rehanna, and the boys had spent their final night. Once there, he opened the bag and started to cry more. He smelled their clothes, called out their names. He couldn't breathe, and he was still in shock, thinking to himself, "Is this real? Are they gone?"

Soon after, he had to return to the hospital to sign the release forms for their bodies. The Turkish government had arranged to transport them to Kobani. Abdullah was filling out the paperwork when big, burly security officers arrived.

"We have to go to the airport right now," one of the officers told Abdullah.

"I'm not leaving without my bag of clothes. I need to go back to the hotel to get them."

"We'll send someone to the hotel for the bag. It will be there when you get to the airport. Don't worry. Let's go."

I spoke with Abdullah at the airport. He was distraught. The clothes were not there.

"I'm not leaving without those clothes," he said to me. I could hear him arguing with someone, asking, "Where are the clothes? I'm not leaving until I get that bag." But the plane was waiting, and they assured him that the bag would be sent to Kobani. When he landed in Urfa, a small city near Kobani on the Turkish border, Abdullah phoned me again.

"Fatima, I don't know what's happening," he said. "There were so many people waiting, and now I'm in a police escort. I'm grateful. But where was all this help when my family was alive?" Apparently, his expired passport and lack of UN card were no longer obstacles. The authorities treated him with the dignity and humanity that he and his wife and children had been denied for so many years—dignity that millions of refugees were still being denied.

Abdullah started to cry again.

"Am I in a dream? Am I still in that water? Was it a nightmare? Am I really talking to you?" His questions made my heart burn.

"I'm seeing a procession of cars and an ambulance. Where am I? What is happening?"

"يرحمن الله حقيقة ايه ،عبدالله, *Ayh haqiqa, Allah yerhamon,* Abdullah, it's real. God rest them in peace."

"We're at the *bab* now," he said, meaning at the gate to Kobani. But I had to wonder if in his current state, Abdullah meant something different. I would have done anything to be there with him. We talked on the phone constantly, but mostly I had to make do once again with the media reports. The cameras followed Abdullah's entire journey to Kobani. Later that day, I watched as the three coffins were loaded onto a plane and flown to Urfa. There, the coffins were unloaded from the plane and placed into an ambulance for another escorted procession to the Martyrs' Cemetery in Kobani. Before the bodies were removed from the ambulance, a photographer snapped a photo of Rehanna's anguished father, Shikho, grasping tiny Alan's shoulders in his big hands, the white shroud I'd dreamt about pulled back, revealing Alan's beautiful face one last time. Seeing those photos of Rehanna's father with Alan made me weep for Rehanna's family and for our father in Damascus. He could not possibly travel through a war zone in one day to get to Kobani in time to say his goodbyes. He would have to watch from afar, just like my family.

With the rest of the world, my family watched the media footage of the burial ceremony. I looked at those video clips and photos again and again, straining to identify my relatives in the crowds and watching my grieving brother repeat his call to the world to help other refugees, the same message he'd expressed to me since the beginning of the war. Afterward, a photographer followed Abdullah to his family's home, where Ghalib spent the majority of his first few years, where Alan was born. Now, less than a year after Abdullah's family had escaped ISIS's Siege of Kobani, the photographer captured Abdullah walking alone down their street against a backdrop of rubble that had once been our neighbours' homes. Abdullah looked as if he belonged among the destruction. He was a wreck of a man.

Abdullah and Rehanna's house had survived ISIS's brutal siege. Though the walls were cracked and peppered with holes from mortar shells, the house still stood. Many of our relatives, young and old, lived in that single dwelling. And now it was packed with mourners. Abdullah returned to his family's bedroom, which still contained Ghalib and Alan's toys. The cameraman visited the bedroom and took photos of Abdullah beside the bed, which was covered with those toys. In one photograph, Abdullah holds a bright stuffed doll, a Sesame Street character with grinning, giant red lips. The photographer captured a hint of a smile on his skinny face, as if he had travelled back in time to a happy memory. Among the toys on that bed, I spotted a pair of baby shoes that I had bought for baby Ghalib and brought to Sham from Canada on my last visit in 2011.

I spoke with Abdullah later that evening. He told me that before he had flown back to Kobani, the Turkish president, Recep Tayyip Erdogan, and his wife, as well as the prime minister, Ahmet Davutoglu, had all called to offer him not just their condolences but even Turkish citizenship.

"I'm grateful that they helped my family to be buried in their homeland, but what good is all this attention now?" Abdullah said. "It's too late for my family."

A few days later, an official called to say that the bag containing his wife's and boys' clothes was waiting at the *bab*. Abdullah was filled with relief. But when he called me an hour later, he was distressed and crying.

"They gave me a bag filled with children's clothes and shoes, but they're not Alan's and Ghalib's clothes. They looked similar—the same colours—but they're new clothes and everything is so big. Some of those clothes still have tags on them. And there's nothing of Rehanna's. I refused to take that bag. I said, 'Find their clothes.' I need those clothes. It would have taken ten minutes to walk to the hotel. I should have gone then. How could they do this to me? What happened to that bag?"

Abdullah could not be consoled. Rehanna and the boys had slipped from his grasp. Now this last keepsake of them was gone too.

PART

THREE

Chapter 11

ما حدا بيقطف ورد إذا بيزرع شوك

Ma hada beyktof ward iza bizra' shouk

Nobody Gets Flowers by Planting Thorns

During those terrible days, my son, Alan, and Rocco were working tirelessly to keep me upright, putting food in front of me, begging me to eat, to sleep, to not wither away. But it wasn't working. I didn't eat. I didn't sleep. I wanted to disappear. I didn't want to face the media requests for interviews. I had to force myself to talk to my friends, who wanted nothing more than to offer condolences and support. I just wanted to be alone with my despair.

My family and friends arranged a beautiful memorial service in Vancouver on September 5 for Rehanna, Ghalib, and Alan. More than two hundred people showed up at Harbour Centre, so many that there wasn't enough room for all of them. My only request was for a bouquet of white flowers and many white balloons. My friends and my son gave beautiful speeches in tribute to Rehanna and the boys, as well as to all the refugees who had died because of the war. Alan capped off his tribute to his aunt and cousins with this simple, beautiful message: "We are all one, regardless of where we come from."

Afterward, many of the mourners joined my family, each of them holding a white balloon. Together, we walked down the city streets to the waterfront. At the harbour, we released the balloons into the sky, and as I tossed the bouquet of white flowers into the water, I prayed for peace in the world. I was deeply moved by the outpouring of love and support from my family, my friends, and from complete strangers. But I was still in shock and longed to be with the rest of my family, especially Abdullah. I had made a promise to my mother that I would take care of Abdullah. It was the last promise I had pledged to her before she died. But I couldn't even take care of myself. And there was no way that my family would let me risk my life to travel to Kobani. The only thing I could do to honour my mother's request was to keep an eye on Abdullah from afar.

I called my cousins in Kobani to ask how he was doing. They told me that he had been sleeping beside the graves of his wife and children every night. One evening, my cousin told me that Abdullah had retreated to his family's little house next door. The house was still covered in dust and rubble from the bombings. Earlier that night, she had heard sobbing coming from his bedroom. She approached the doorway and saw Abdullah sitting on the bed, lit by a flickering candle, surrounded by his boys' clothes and toys. He was calling out his family's names, holding their clothes to his nose and crying, "Where did you go? Why did you leave me alone? وينكن يا روح بابا، *Wainkon ya roh baba? Ya alb baba?*" It means "Where are you, my heart, my soul? Now that I've lost you, I've lost my heart and soul. What am I now?"

"He can't be left alone like that, in that dusty room, surrounded by their clothes and toys, filled with reminders of everything he has lost," my cousin said in a whisper so that Abdullah wouldn't overhear her.

In those first days after the tragedy, Ghalib and Alan weren't just visions in Abdullah's imagination. The photograph of Alan remained alive in millions of minds. Many artists created their own interpretation of that photograph as a tribute—on murals, on paintings, and on statues—and to serve as permanent reminders to never forget, to never go back to sleep. Refugees and activists also embraced the picture of Alan, putting it on protest signs and on T-shirts, rallying the world to prevent more senseless deaths. Heads of state in many countries weighed in, offering sympathies and promises of help and pleas to other global leaders to do the same.

My home country of Canada was in the final month of a federal election campaign, and that picture of Alan was immediately evoked by parties running against Prime Minister Stephen Harper. Justin Trudeau, at the time the leader of the Liberal Party, pledged that if he was elected, he would take in 25,000 refugees by year's end. He chastised Harper for not doing enough to help Syrian refugees seek safety in Canada. On the day of the tragedy, Harper was campaigning in my home province of British Columbia. The following day—the same day that I did my press conference—he held his own press conference, saying, "We are doing everything and we will do more of everything" for refugees seeking asylum. As if doing everything equates to accepting a mere 1,002 Syrian refugees. And though his immigration minister told reporters on the day after the tragedy that the numbers had suddenly increased to 2,300, Harper continued to provide only a vague pledge to take in 10,000 people from the Middle East.

Among the countries around the world, Sweden and Germany deserve the greatest thanks, because they began to resettle Syrian refugees long before that tragic night. German chancellor Angela Merkel received my deepest thanks for reacting to the tragedy by throwing open the country's borders to every single asylum-seeking refugee. Her government pledged to take in up to 500,000 people each year. Austria also agreed to open its doors, and Merkel called on other countries to do the same, or at least provide safe passage to the countries that were accepting refugees. Her message was meant for the Central European countries standing in the way of the refugees trying to reach Northern Europe. Hungary had become a particularly dangerous bottleneck after its government refused to allow refugees into the country; a huge razor-wire fence had been built to stop the northward flow of refugees.

My nephew Yasser was one of the many refugees trapped inside Hungary at that very moment, facing his own horrors as he tried to reach Germany. He was in a makeshift prison—a large, fenced-in pen in the middle of a forest—with many other refugees. Occasionally the guards threw water and sandwiches over the fence. But the sandwiches contained a mystery meat that the refugees suspected contained pork. At first, they would eat the bread and toss the meat back. But the meat attracted feral dogs that would bark and snarl on the other side of the fence, terrorizing the refugees even more.

Yasser and a number of other refugees were eventually herded onto a bus without being told where they would be taken. Hours later, when he and the others were ordered off the bus, he found himself walking through a gate into Austria. An Austrian couple beckoned to Yasser and a family on the bus, speaking to them through gestures—eating, showering, laying a head on a pillow. It appeared they were offering them a place to eat and shower and sleep. It was like a fairy tale. The couple fed them and gave them soft towels and fragrant soap for their hot showers. Yasser called his mom, Shireen, to let her know he had arrived in Austria, safe and comparatively sound.

"But I need to get to Germany," Yasser said to his mom. "They've been so kind and I don't want to be rude, but I can't stay here."

"Do they speak English?"

"Yes."

"Then call your Auntie Fatima," Shireen advised. "She'll explain everything to them."

Yasser called me and recounted his incredible story. I asked him if I could talk to the couple. He passed the phone to the wife. I thanked her for taking such good care of my nephew. I explained that he wanted to get to Germany, and then I told them about our family's tragedy.

"You're the aunt of the boy on the beach? The Canadian woman?" she exclaimed. "Your story is all over the news."

She said that Yasser was welcome to stay with them for as long as he liked. I explained that he wanted to be reunited with his uncle Mohammad, who was still in a camp in Germany. The next morning, the couple took Yasser to the train station and bought him a ticket for Germany. I saw some of that footage of those refugees pouring into Austria and Germany. I cried so many bittersweet tears as I looked at the photos and videos. Abdullah saw it all too.

"Are you watching the news?" he asked me during one of our calls. "Look what that picture of Alan did. All the borders are starting to open across Europe. He saved their lives, *Alhamdulillah*. Thank God. أخيراً الدنيا صحيت, *Akheeran aldounia sihyat*. Finally the world has woken up."

I found myself looking for the faces of Rehanna, Ghalib, and Alan among those weary refugees arriving in Germany. It made no sense to do such a thing. But death makes no sense, especially the death of innocent children. When you are in the depths of grief, it seems utterly absurd that people are alive one day, and then the next, they are gone.

Every minute of every hour of those terrible first weeks—everything I saw, everything I experienced—provided an entirely new set of what-ifs and if-onlys. If only the Canadian government's policies had been less restrictive. If only the family had made that sea crossing successfully, that photograph of Alan would never have happened. It would not be there to provide a call to the world. Greece would probably have given Abdullah's family safe passage, as it had been doing for the past months for many refugees. But Abdullah and his family would still have had to traverse those inhospitable and perilous Central European countries.

Perhaps Abdullah's family would have been trapped at one border or another, with thousands of other refugees, penned in like animals inside a high fence, surrounded by an armoury of men with weapons at the ready. They may have been sent back to Turkey. But they would have been alive.

"You will drive yourself crazy if you keep doing that," said Rocco in response to one of my never-ending what-if rants. "You can't turn back the clock. Just eat something and get some sleep," he begged, sticking another plate of food in front of my face. Sleep was impossible. I could not silence or even slow my racing mind.

In Canada, the tragedy continued to stir up partisan arguments among the various political parties in the lead-up to the national election. As a result, everyone was pointing the finger at Prime Minister Stephen Harper and his Conservative government. Within a few weeks, with the election looming, he would be forced to temporarily waive the UN referral requirements for privately sponsored Syrian refugees. It was good news, but it was still too little, too late.

Around the world, the photograph of my nephew had galvanized the public to press their politicians. Human rights organizations and citizens held vigils and memorials for Alan and the refugees, both living and dead, and many charity groups experienced a surge in donations. Words will never be enough to express my gratitude to all the people who took action and made many personal sacrifices to help those in need.

But fraudulent charities also sprang up on the Internet, using the image of my nephew to satisfy their own greed. I saw one of these fraudsters on a Facebook post. The link went to a UK-based site that had collected $170,000 in just two days. It featured a family photo of Alan and Ghalib that I had posted, and the website was made to look as if it had been created by my family. But my family didn't have a charity. My family had nothing to do with that website. I sent a text message to the man listed as the host of the website, asking to know where that money was going to be spent. I also told him that he needed to change his website and the picture of my nephews so that it didn't appear as if it had been created by my family. If he didn't, I said, he would have to take the website down. His response was the typical schoolyard bully's reply: "Make me." And then *I* was blocked from his Twitter and Facebook accounts.

Just as sickening was that detractors of my family were also quick to react. Among them were US politician Michele Bachmann and an Australian politician named Cory Bernardi, both of whom twisted my words from my first press conference to suit their own warped views. They cited my mention of Abdullah's need for dental treatment, saying that Abdullah had risked his family's life just to get dental care in Europe. Other critics claimed that our family was trying to profit from the tragedy. Did these people have no sympathy and compassion to spare for my family and millions of refugees? Did they have any idea what it's like not to have a piece of bread to feed their families?

After reading one post that called my brother a selfish man who would "Kill his own family," I called my *baba* in tears.

"*Habibti*, sweetheart, it doesn't matter what those strangers think," he said. "Abdullah was an incredible father. He gave those kids a lifetime of love. Those people don't understand. ما حدا بيقطف ورد إذا بيزرع شوك, *Ma hada beyktof ward iza bizra' shouk*. Nobody gets flowers by planting thorns."

ISIS was also quick to use the photograph of Alan to support its beastly ideology, saying that my family deserved their fate because they had tried to escape the Middle East for Europe.

Abdullah didn't know that hate and misinformation were spreading across the world. And even if he had, it wouldn't have mattered to him. He was in a much darker place than even the loudest haters could have imagined. The fact that Abdullah was once again back in the war zone made me even crazier with worry. Kobani was still a dangerous place, but to Abdullah, it didn't matter anymore that he was surrounded by the threat of war. People were attempting to rebuild their homes and their lives, but Abdullah had no family and no life left to rebuild.

Nechirvan Barzani, the prime minister of the Kurdistan Regional Government (KRG), had reached out to Abdullah, inviting him to stay in Erbil, the capital of Kurdistan, an autonomous region in northeastern Iraq. I tried to convince Abdullah to accept the offer and go to Kurdistan, at least for a few weeks, until he needed to be back in Kobani for the memorial, which happened forty days after death. I could not get out of my mind the picture of Abdullah sleeping beside his family's graves. But Abdullah wanted to stay. Maybe he felt at home among so many ghosts. Maybe a ghost family was better than no family at all.

The constant watching and waiting from afar made me feel beyond useless. It was as if I were permanently strapped into a roller coaster that forced me up, down, and upside down, but always returned me to the exact same place, where I'd start all over again. I was desperate to see Abdullah in the flesh. I was desperate to be with my whole family.

That opportunity came when a citizens action group called Avaaz contacted me, asking me to fly to Brussels to speak at a September 14 meeting of UNHCR, the UN Refugee Agency. They wanted me to deliver the politicians a petition signed by 1.2 million people calling for the EU to take action on the Syrian refugee crisis. I was incapable of travelling on my own. I could not even feed myself. So Rocco told Avaaz that I would go, but only if they would sponsor my son, Alan, to accompany me. He also told them that I was unwilling to express a partisan political view about the war in Syria: I was there to speak for the refugees, not for a political viewpoint, so I would not take sides. They agreed and also helped pay for my flights to see my family in Germany and Turkey. We even had a tentative plan to bring Abdullah from Kobani to Istanbul so that we could be together. The plan mobilized me. With only a few days to prepare for my journey, I scrambled to get ready. We were due to leave for Brussels on September 11, and then we'd be in Germany a few days later. Alan and I gathered things to bring to Germany for Mohammad and Yasser, and also to the rest of my family in Turkey.

Things moved quickly from the moment I stepped on European soil. Just one day after arriving, I was shuttled to media interviews and a private meeting with the foreign minister of Luxembourg and the president of the Council of the European Union. On the third day, I had to speak at the UN meeting. If I had not been so exhausted and gutted, I probably would have been shaking in my shoes thinking about what I might possibly say to all those powerful, important politicians, including António Guterres, then the UN High Commissioner for Refugees, and Federica Mogherini, the vice-president of the UN's European Commission.

Maybe I was still in shock, but I felt no stage fright. I simply stood before these strangers in their suits and spoke from my heart, repeating the message that had now become a mantra: please open your hearts and doors to refugees, or at least give them safe passage to prevent them from drowning; please sit down at the table with all the world leaders and share your ideas on finding a peaceful way to stop the Syrian war, and until then, open your borders.

That whole experience is a blur. After the meeting, I was placed in a receiving line and each diplomat filed past and shook my hand. I began to understand my brother's confusion and astonishment at being thrust in the spotlight, at suddenly being treated with respect and compassion, at finally seeing the world wake up to the refugee crisis and take it seriously.

Some of the politicians had tears in their eyes, hugged me to their chests, and took pictures with *me,* a hairdresser. Many of the diplomats promised to do more for the refugees, pledging that my family's tragedy would be the last. They handed me their business cards, saying that I should not hesitate to contact them if I needed anything. I thanked them all and repeated my message.

A few months later, I contacted some of these influencers to ask how I could be of further service in support of refugees. Some responded; most did not. It seemed they had gone back to sleep. I wish I could go back in time, knowing what I know now, so that I could deliver my message more powerfully.

After that first, otherworldly meeting, I was taken to the hotel and ferried from one room to the next to do more interviews. In one conversation, the reporter referred to Alan as "Aylan."

"His name is Alan, actually," I said.

"Yes, but the world knows him as Aylan, so we need to continue with that," she responded.

I rarely cried as I recalled Abdullah's account of the tragedy, I suppose because I was exhausted and disoriented from being in a foreign world, both physically and metaphorically. In that European world of palaces and church spires and monuments to European power old and new, I felt as if I were in a fairy tale—the kind that turns into a nightmare.

Later that day, Alan and I flew to Frankfurt, Germany. When we arrived, I found out that Abdullah had accepted the offer of asylum in Erbil, Kurdistan. That meant I could see him! I just had to get a plane ticket from Turkey to Erbil, to finish my trip.

Alan and I planned to meet with my brother and nephew for lunch. But the taxi driver told me that Mohammad's shelter in Heidelberg was not too far from my hotel, and he could take us directly there. I couldn't wait to see my brother. En route, the taxi driver discussed the flood of refugees. The taxi pulled up to a security booth adjacent to the refugee shelter, which resembled a housing project. (It was actually a former US army base, dating back to the 1940s.) I wasn't allowed into the compound, but a security guard agreed to look for my brother. I got out of the taxi to stretch my legs and have a closer look at the shelter. On the other side of the chain-link fence was a small children's playground. A half-dozen skinny refugee children in dirty clothes were running about and playing on a squeaky swing set. They were happy, but many of them were coughing and looked sickly, shivering in their T-shirts. Though it was still only mid-September, there was an autumn chill in the air and the sky was grey and gloomy. I started to cry. Once again, I had to wonder, "Why them? Why us? How did we get here?"

The security guy returned and said that Mohammad couldn't leave the shelter without permission papers, so the driver took us back to the hotel. I texted my brother and Yasser with the hotel's address, telling them to take taxis once they were able to leave and that I'd reimburse them. My nephew Yasser was living at a separate shelter for children in Heidelberg, not too far from Mohammad's camp. Yasser was the first to arrive at the hotel. By then, the clouds had burst, and it was pouring rain outside. Yasser was soaking wet, wearing just a very light T-shirt and shaking from head to toe.

"Oh my God. Why no jacket?" I asked, hugging him long and hard.

"ما تاكلي هم خالتي, *Ma takli ham khalti*. Don't worry, Auntie. I'm used to it," he said.

Alan immediately opened the suitcase and gave Yasser a jacket and clothes. Mohammad arrived in a similar state, and so we went through the same ritual. I told them both to take hot showers. Mohammad had not had a shower like that since leaving Damascus in 2012.

"Let's go eat," I said. I wanted so badly to put food in their bellies.

On the streets of Frankfurt, I saw many of my Syrian people, some even begging for food. "I'm hungry, I'm tired. I can't walk anymore," I heard a small boy crying.

"Auntie, what's the name of your boy?" I asked his mother.

"Khalid," she said.

"Why are you crying?" I asked Khalid. He was too shy to answer and hid behind his mom's skirt.

"We're staying in a refugee camp," his mom explained. "We have to fight every morning just to get a piece of bread with jam. There's not enough food, so I have to give my kids all the food." I could not turn away from this boy. He could have been my nephew.

"Come with me," I said. We went down the street to a vendor who sold Middle Eastern food. I bought them shawarmas.

"*Allah ya'tiki al-siha w yikhali wladik.* God give you health and bless your kids," said the woman.

I told Mohammad and Yasser that I would buy them anything they wanted for lunch.

"Anything but canned tuna fish," Mohammad said.

"I think I could eat a whole cow," Yasser said, laughing.

We came upon a restaurant with big, fat, glistening rotisserie chickens in the windows.

"We've been dreaming of roasted chicken for so many months," said Mohammad. "I could eat an entire chicken myself."

"Oh my God, yes," said Yasser.

I bought them chicken and kebabs, and I watched them savour every single bite of that food. My heart was happy. It was a beautiful moment.

"Why are you just sitting there, grinning at us? Eat!" said Mohammad.

"I'm too happy to eat," I said. "Tell me what it's like in the shelters."

"Auntie, you don't want to know. And I don't want to sound ungrateful, but there are too many refugees packed in. Everyone is living on top of each other. But this is temporary. It will get better," said Yasser.

"The food is terrible," said Mohammad. "We have to line up and wait for hours, even for the simplest request."

I knew that beneath Mohammad's gripes, he was missing his family so much. It could take up to a year for him to bring his family to join him in Germany. In many ways, his situation was worse than in Istanbul; even with the worst job possible in Turkey, he came home each night to his family. After Mohammad had left Turkey, Ghouson had given birth to their newest child, a boy named Sherwan. But Mohammad hadn't even met his youngest child yet in the flesh. It must have been excruciating for him to not be able to hug and kiss his baby boy and see his family.

After lunch, we walked down the busy street and went to a supermarket, where I bought Mohammad sharp scissors and clippers so that he could cut his hair and perhaps find work at the shelter. They returned with us to the hotel and stayed there until curfew at eight p.m.

The next day Mohammad and Yasser came to the hotel again. We did two German media interviews and then we went out to eat. The weather was still chilly, but the sun had broken out from behind the clouds. We went to a Turkish restaurant and sat outside on the patio, just like we used to do in Damascus. I ordered way too much food, and when the restaurant manager found out that Mohammad and Yasser were Syrian refugees, the kind man piled the food even higher. We spent hours on that patio, talking about our family's tragedy—it still didn't feel real to us—and remembering life in Damascus before the war. We were there for so long that the waiters began to stack the seats up around us. We apologized for overstaying our welcome, but the owner insisted there was no need to rush; we could stay as long as we liked.

At the bus station, we said our tearful goodbyes and I watched my nephew climb onto his bus with his take-away bag of food. Mohammad decided to stay in the hotel with us that night; he got a friend to sign him back in at the shelter so that he would not get into trouble. Alan told Mohammad that he was welcome to sleep in his bed, but Mohammad insisted on taking the floor, saying, "I'm used to it. And everything is so clean here. I'm perfectly fine."

As soon as the lights went out, Mohammad started to talk to me.

"ياالله ليش هيك صار فينا, *Ya Allah leish heik saar fina?* Oh God, why is this happening to us, sister? Why to Abdullah? Why only to the poor?" He could not put his mind to rest.

"Brother, we can't change it now. *Inshallah*, everything will get better."

Despite Mohammad's laments, I think I had my first sound sleep in many months that night, with my son and my well-fed brother in the same room. Mohammad and I had not slept in the same room since we were small kids in the house in Damascus. It was so hard to say goodbye to my big brother that next morning. I felt that I had failed him and Abdullah by not being able to secure them asylum in Canada. So much was still uncertain: I didn't know when I'd see Mohammad again or when he would be able to reunite with his family. Alan was flying back to Vancouver that morning, while I was continuing on to Turkey and Erbil. I hugged Alan hard, feeling so blessed to have such a beautiful son, but I was also very uncertain about the next stages of my journey. As soon as Alan left my side, I felt unmoored all over again.

When I arrived in Istanbul, I texted Hivron and told her where I was staying. Shortly after, she arrived with her kids and a bag of food.

"Open this," she said, her eyes sparkling with that old childhood mischief. The bag contained two pieces of "broasted" chicken with a delicious side of creamy garlic sauce, my favourite Syrian "fast food"—like KFC, but much, much better.

"Where did you find this?" I asked Hivron.

"A Syrian franchise just opened in Istanbul for all the homesick Syrians. I know how much you love it," Hivron said.

I savoured that food while Hivron and the kids watched me, smiling with satisfaction, as if *I* were a refugee. I had a beautiful evening with my nieces and nephews. Then Hivron sent them home so that we could have time alone. She was sleeping over that night, and I was tired from the travel. But Hivron wanted to talk about her own horrific Mediterranean crossings, attempted during the same month that Abdullah and his family were trying to cross. On Hivron's first try, the women had been separated from the men, loaded into different trucks, and then sent to a boat by themselves. There had been a frantic period when Hivron and her husband didn't know if they'd see each other again. When they got to the boat, Hivron refused to board. After the family reunited, they tried to travel together by boat again. But they were forced to turn back—by patrol boats and then the elements.

On their third attempt to flee, they hid in the trees near the beach, and the kids had collected stones while they waited for the smugglers.

"What are you making?" Hivron had asked her kids.

"قبر, *Qabr*," they'd responded. "It's a baby's grave."

My sister's hair had stood up in fright.

When the boat showed up, it was just a flimsy dinghy. The smugglers tried to herd the refugees onto the boat with sticks, but Hivron held her ground and refused to go.

"I would never attempt that crossing again," she said to me in the hotel room. "After that tragedy, never ever, even for a million dollars. It's not worth the risk."

"*Inshallah*, the German government will approve your resettlement soon, and you'll be reunited," I said.

Just as I was about to fall asleep, Hivron started to weep. I shot right up in the bed and started to cry too.

"Fatima, I want to confess something about Abdullah," she said. "نادمانة, *Ana nadmaneh.* It's my deepest regret. After Rehanna and the boys fled Kobani, Abdullah asked if they could stay with me until they found a place of their own. Even though it hurt, I said, 'I'm sorry, brother, there's no room for all of you.'"

My poor sister. I tried to console her. "If you had let them stay, both of your families might have been evicted. You couldn't risk that."

"I know. But I think I broke his heart."

"No, sister. He understands. He's not upset about it. He found a place to live eventually." No matter what I said, it did little to ease her pain.

"Look at where we came from and where we are now. Why is this happening to us? وحياة الله تعبنا, *Wihyat Allah ta'abneh.* I swear to God, I am tired."

"*Hada nasib.* It's fate. *Inshallah*, it will get better soon."

Eventually, we drifted off to sleep in tears.

The next day, I had to do an interview with a Dutch broadcaster;

then Ghouson and her kids came over with a million questions about their dad: "How is Mohammad? Is he skinny? How's his health? How's Yasser? What's Germany like?" Maha arrived shortly after. It was a relief to have much of my family reunited under one roof again, but still, the visit was painful, with all of us asking one another "Why?" over and over.

I had another mission in Istanbul. I wanted to visit Abdullah and Rehanna's home. I had seen many photos, but I wanted to see that place for myself. I wanted to sit down on their green couch and cry my heart out. The couch that my nephews had sat upon so many times—the one that I'd seen them laugh and dance upon; the one in the photograph with the white teddy bear between them.

Maha and her daughter took me there. A new Syrian refugee family from Aleppo was living in the home—a couple and their four-year-old son. We arrived and introduced ourselves, but they knew who we were and welcomed us inside right away.

"I've heard a lot about your family from the neighbours," the women said. "Everyone said they were a loving family and talked about the father, how he used to take the two boys with him everywhere. الله يرحمن, *Allah yerhamon*. God rest them in peace."

My eyes were immediately drawn to the green couch. Maha and I sat down, putting our hands on the cushions, imagining the boys there. We were silent, overcome by grief, as we looked around. I could see the boys chasing each other and playing in the corners. I could hear them laughing and singing while Rehanna cooked their meals and sang along. The Syrian woman went to the closet and pulled out a plastic bag. In it was the big white teddy bear from the photo that Abdullah had sent me. The woman had hidden it away after she moved in, just in case Abdullah wanted it. Then she pulled out a box of my nephews' toys—plastic dump trucks and a number of others that I had come to know well from photos and our video calls, including the Teletubby with a missing eye, a stuffed monkey (one of Ghalib's favourites), and a stuffed dog sticking its tongue out (Alan's favourite).

"Please, take the toys to your brother," the woman said.

I didn't know what to do, so I called Abdullah in Erbil.

"I know what it means for a refugee family to have toys for their children," he said. "Leave them for that boy. It would make me happy to know that he's playing with them. I brought some of their toys from Kobani."

"*Hatta alkalib?* Even the dog with the tongue?" I asked.

"*Ahhh, mishan Allah geebih.* Oh God, bring that. Alan loved that toy so much. He played with it all the time. He'd put his little hands on my cheeks and turn my head so that we were face to face, eye to eye. Then he'd hold out that stuffed dog and talk in his baby talk, like that dog had something important to say."

Abdullah started to cry. "Please bring that dog. And the monkey. And the truck," he said.

After I said goodbye to Abdullah, I had a final look around. Ghalib's tricycle sat in the corner. The couch and mattress took up the majority of the space. The only festive decoration in the room was a birthday banner hanging on the wall, showing a big sparkle-covered birthday cake, and dangling below it, the multi-coloured words "*Iyiki Dogdun,*" Turkish for "Happy Birthday." Abdullah had hung that decoration months earlier for Alan's second birthday party, on June 6, and for Ghalib's fourth birthday the following month.

I thanked the Syrian woman many times, and I took the decoration and the few toys with me. As I boarded the flight to Erbil, the toys felt heavy in my suitcase. I wondered if bringing the mementos to Abdullah would help him heal or cause him even more pain.

Chapter 12

متل رفة العين

Mitl raffit al'ain

In the Blink of an Eye

Abdullah was waiting for me when I got off the plane in Erbil. He looked frail and haunted. His clothes—khaki pants and shirt, like a military uniform—hung from his body.

"I'm so sorry" were the first words from my mouth, as I tried not to crush Abdullah with my hug.

"*La ilaha ill Allah.* God is the only deity," he responded.

It was such a relief to be with my brother again. But I could not resist worrying aloud about his gaunt appearance.

"Don't worry, sister. Lots of people are looking out for me here," he said, even Prime Minister Nechirvan Barzani, whom he'd met shortly after arriving in Kurdistan.

"We talked for an hour," Abdullah said. "قلبه طيّب, *Albo tayyib.* He's very kind and good-hearted, like a brother. He promised to help me with anything I need. I'm so grateful to him."

The Kurdish Regional Government had generously provided Abdullah with a room in a posh hotel. The KRG treated him like a VIP, assigning him a jack-of-all-trades liaison, who acted as his driver and personal assistant. They had planned many activities for Abdullah, including a meeting with Masoud Barzani, the president of Kurdistan. But the luxuries were lost on Abdullah, once again forcing him to wonder, "Why now, when it's too late?"

Abdullah and I visited President Barzani soon after I arrived. He asked Abdullah to tell him everything that had happened to his family since the war had started, and he sat quietly while Abdullah recounted his family's story. When Barzani said anything at all, he was soft-spoken and kind. When Abdullah told him what had happened to his teeth, Barzani was upset and vowed to get him dental treatment.

"I can't wait for you to have teeth again, so that you can eat and smile like you used to," I told Abdullah after our visit with Mr. Barzani.

But Abdullah's mind was elsewhere. "I don't care about my teeth. I wish I had the power to help all the children in the world. All the things I couldn't do for my kids, I want to do for those refugees. Can you take us to a refugee camp?" Abdullah asked the driver.

The KRG driver was happy to fulfill the request. In that first week of my two-week stay, we visited seven different refugee camps in various parts of Kurdistan. The Kurdistan camps didn't receive much funding from global charities. But the Kurdish government did its best to accommodate and respect the displaced. They had opened the door to refugees, and by 2015, they said that 1.7 million refugees were living in Kurdistan. Some of the camps were quite large. I was surprised that many of them resembled typical Arab villages. They had refugee-run shops, including hair salons and marketplaces under billowing blue and white tents. At least some people could work and make a bit of an independent life for themselves.

The only time I saw Abdullah truly smile his toothless grin was when we met the children at those camps. Each time, he went straight to the playgrounds.

"*Habibati.* Sweethearts, what do you need most of all?" he asked them, as they clamoured around him.

"Uncle, we want to go to school," one child called out.

"Yes, we miss school," chimed in many other kids. "But we don't have school supplies. We need backpacks with school supplies."

"I'll see what I can do," said Abdullah.

When we got back to the hotel, Abdullah told his contact about what he had heard from the children. "I want to bring those backpacks to the kids, so I can see the smiles on their faces," Abdullah said.

The government honoured the request. We returned to the camp with backpacks filled with school supplies. The kids came running and formed a circle around Abdullah as he handed out those backpacks.

"Thank you, Abu Alan," the kids cheered.

Among them, Abdullah spotted a little boy, and my brother's smile beamed.

"Oh my God, sister, doesn't he look like Alan? Sweetheart, you are like an angel."

The boy did look quite like Alan. But I think Abdullah was projecting the image he most wanted to see.

At another, smaller camp of approximately two hundred refugees, the kids told Abdullah that they couldn't attend school because the camp was too far away. "We need buses to take them there and back," said the parents. So Abdullah talked to the mayor of that city about it, and the mayor took care of it.

Trying to get Abdullah to leave the camp was like pulling a child from a teeter-totter. On the car ride back to Erbil, he said, "I want to open a school for children in Kobani, and I want to name it after Alan and Ghalib. I want that school to be shaped like a big, colourful lifeboat. And I want to start a charity to help refugee kids everywhere. Children are innocent. They are the most beautiful thing in the world."

When the Kurdish government said that they might be able to help sponsor Abdullah's dream project, it became his only interest, aside from seeking a stop to the Syrian war, something that not even the biggest power brokers of the world had been able to do for more than four years.

"We need to be the voice of those people, Fatima," Abdullah said to me. "We need to help them in whatever way we can."

Life at the hotel in Erbil was a stark contrast to the camps. We returned from each day's refugee camp tour to have tea or coffee among the many wealthy tourists and business people in the hotel's lobby. Most of the time, Abdullah and I sat in silence, lost in our own worlds, drinking our expensive coffees. Every time an attentive waiter approached to refill our seemingly bottomless cups, we'd say, "*Shukran*. Thank you so much." We'd say the same thing whenever someone recognized Abdullah and came over to offer condolences.

The Kurdish citizenry took the tragic deaths of Rehanna, Ghalib, and Alan to heart. I can understand why. Kurds have faced enormous hardship and persecution throughout history, including during Saddam Hussein's reign of terror and genocide, which still haunted many of them. Naturally, they embraced Abdullah's tragedy as one of their own. And the tragedy generated constant media coverage in Kurdistan. The Kurdish people were struck by the photograph of Alan, perhaps more than citizens of many other countries. And that photograph was everywhere:

on the TV at the hotel bar, on posters throughout the city, at the refugee camps, and at every event we attended. We met many Kurds whose lives had been shattered by war, racism, and intolerance—at the refugee camps, and during the various excursions hosted by the KRG. Each of their heartbreaking stories could fill a book.

Some people asked Abdullah for financial aid, and he wanted to help all of them—to pay for a life-saving surgery for a child or grandparent, to get a family a house before the cold winter came. In their eyes, Abdullah was a rich and powerful man now. They didn't know that the food keeping him alive and the clothes on his back had been paid for by me and by the KRG. They didn't know that the only money he had was the two Turkish coins in his pocket, which had survived that brutal night at sea and which he carried everywhere as a memorial to Ghalib. They didn't know that if the KRG hadn't taken Abdullah under its wing, he would have remained under the charge of his relatives in Kobani, who could barely feed and shelter themselves. They didn't know that in many ways, my brother had less than nothing. He had the power of a man who had been drowning at sea for weeks.

Throughout that time, the local and international media followed Abdullah's every step, requesting interviews. As with everything else, he felt obligated to accept any request. I accompanied him to a few of those interviews. The English and European media would sometimes bring Arabic translators, but too often they mistranslated Abdullah's words. I had to keep interrupting, saying, "No, Abdullah didn't say that. He said this." The media continued to refer to the boat that had capsized as an inflatable dinghy, and Abdullah didn't try to correct them. The only time he braced and spoke up was when the media called his son Aylan.

Abdullah was just like a wishbone, with everyone pulling at him. It was only a matter of time before the constant pressure broke him in half.

We had another goal on our agenda: visit the namesake of both of our sons. Alana is a tiny village in the Alana Valley, northeast of Erbil, near the Iranian border. The KRG kindly arranged for us to visit the area, and it was by far the most extraordinary of all the fairy-tale places that I would visit on that trip. The landscape was more beautiful than any masterpiece painting I have ever seen. Those mountains and valleys and trees had such varied shades of green. There were rivers and cascading waterfalls everywhere, luminescent, like silk. It was a heavenly moving picture. The village itself looked as if it had been carved out of the mountainside. When we got there, all the locals came rushing to greet our vehicle. We instantly felt at home. The mayor of the town escorted us around, pointing out the Alana School.

"Can you believe this?" whispered Abdullah, his eyes huge.

I can't imagine what was going through his mind. After the village tour, the mayor took us to his house, where the women had been preparing a banquet. I insisted on helping with the cooking and went into the kitchen to find four women preparing a huge Kurdish meal, all harvested from their own gardens and chicken coops and herds of sheep—just like in Kobani. The smells in that kitchen—oh my God. A stew was bubbling in the biggest pot I have ever seen. It was amazing, like a trip back in time.

When the moment came to serve the meal, I insisted on eating like all the locals, the same way my father liked to eat: cross-legged on the floor. Everyone offered their deepest sympathies to Abdullah, and our talk turned to the many hardships that the villagers' families had experienced during the Iraq war, during Saddam Hussein's reign of brutal ethnic cleansing, and under the rule of hostile or indifferent governments going back through many centuries. These villagers still carried the traditions and ideologies of their Kurdish ancestors: they were a multicultural, multi-religious group of people living together in harmony, working the land as peaceful farmers and herders.

The day flew by. With our driver under instructions to return us to Erbil by nightfall, we had to tear ourselves from those good people long before we were ready to do so.

"I could live my whole life in that village," said Abdullah as the car pulled away. "Sister, we could live like we used to when we were kids."

I could hardly blame Abdullah for wanting to go back to the past. We both would have done anything to turn back the hands of time. Instead, we sat in the car and marveled at the living painting of the Alana Valley as we sped to Erbil.

Abdullah asked whether I'd brought Alan and Ghalib's toys back to him. "I need those toys from Istanbul," he said. "I want to touch the things that have Ghalib and Alan's fingerprints on them."

"Brother, I mailed them to Vancouver," I lied.

"Do you think I'm stupid? You mailed them from Turkey?"

He knew the toys were still in my suitcase. But that image of Abdullah in Kobani, looking at his kids' toys, was ingrained in my mind, and I couldn't bring myself to reveal the toys to him. I didn't think he could withstand the memories they would bring back, so I left them in my suitcase.

The next morning, I texted Abdullah and told him to meet me downstairs for coffee. We made our way to the hotel's restaurant, with its big-screen TVs broadcasting the latest horrifying news from Syria. The majority of the hotel guests registered little more than a passing interest in the unfolding events on the news. They seemed entirely removed from all forms of suffering and pain. Even though we were in the Middle East—under those impossibly blue skies, the weather so hot—it felt like a foreign world, a world entirely removed from the humble one we had grown up in, and even more so from the brutal reality of war and poverty. We sat in silence again, overhearing the fashionable tourists and business people ordering their expensive breakfasts, breakfasts that cost more than a refugee makes for an entire week of back-breaking labour.

"What are we doing here?" I asked Abdullah.

"Sister, don't you think I ask myself that question every minute? We could write a book."

"You're right. We should. For Rehanna and the boys. For all the innocent people victimized by war."

His face turned ashen and his eyes filled with tears. I followed his gaze to the TV screen: that photograph of Alan again.

"إبني, *Ibni.* My son. يا روحي يرحمك الله, *Allah yerhamak ya rohi.* Rest in peace, my beloved," Abdullah said. Then he turned to me. "I need to get out of here."

The midday heat was like a brick wall, but the streets were quiet. We didn't speak, we just let our tears run. After a while, we sat down on a bench in a square with a splashing fountain. As the sun shone down on us, I tried to help Abdullah open up.

"Abdullah, what exactly happened that night? You need to talk about it."

Abdullah was silent for a while. Then he spoke. "The waves were too strong. I did everything I could to save them. But it wasn't enough. I couldn't save them, Fatima." Abdullah put his head in his hands and started to sob. "رفة العين متل, *Mitl raffit al'ain.* It happened in the blink of an eye. They were gone."

I knelt down on the ground in front of him and hugged his shins to my chest, his bony knees pressing into my collarbone.

"I can't breathe," he said. "No one can understand our pain unless they walk in our shoes."

I let go and stood up. I took his hand and pulled him up from that bench. We walked back to the hotel and Abdullah went to his room. I wondered if I had gone too far, asked too much. But slowly, over the following days, he shared more details with me, and eventually I was able to see just how traumatic that night had been.

"The boat was too small for all of us," Abdullah said. "The bow was pointed, so there wasn't much space on the floor of the boat. Everyone was quiet as we boarded. Alan was still fast asleep, and Ghalib was half asleep." The Turkish man whom Abdullah had met earlier was at the helm, speaking in gestures as the refugees boarded.

"Rehanna and I sat down at the bow. Ghalib was in my lap, and Alan was in Rehanna's. Right away, the waves were slamming against the boat. It woke up Ghalib and Alan. The sensation of the spray of water on his face made Alan laugh. It made Ghalib cry."

"I held Ghalib to my heart, saying, 'لا تخاف بابا حبيبي, *la tkhaf baba habibi*. Don't be scared, sweetheart.' The waves were so strong and powerful, and the boat was so overloaded that it started to take on water. People started screaming. We were like rag dolls against the thudding waves. In panic, the driver dived off the boat. I was sitting close to the front, but I could reach out with one hand and hold on to the steering wheel. The boat was drifting in the open sea, and I tried to steer it, but I was still holding Ghalib, and Rehanna was holding on to me too."

Abdullah told me the waves overwhelmed the overloaded boat. It capsized, throwing everyone into the sea.

"It was pandemonium in the water. I held Ghalib and Alan and tried to corral them with one arm, and Rehanna was still holding my arm; we had our arms hooked at the elbow. I was using my legs too, trying to hold up the boys with one knee and Rehanna with the other. I kept screaming, 'Breathe!' But the waves kept pummelling us underwater. Rehanna was the first one gone. She kept yelling, 'Save the kids!' Then I couldn't hear her voice anymore. She was gone, just like that," Abdullah said, snapping his fingers. "I could only pray that her life jacket would save her. Each time a wave knocked us underwater, I tried to get under the boys and push them up to the surface, منشان يتنفسوا, *minshan yitnafsoo*, so they could breathe. But as soon I got them back to the surface, a new wave knocked them back under.

"I don't know how long it went on like that. There was a lot of yelling and screaming, but I didn't hear the boys make any sounds. I was yelling to myself, 'Don't die. Please don't die. ياالله ساعِدُن, *Ya Allah sa'idon*. Oh God, help them.'"

Abdullah thought about trying to swim to the shore, but the current was strong and the waves were knocking him sideways; the twinkling lights of the Turkish coastline seemed too far away. He could only hope that bystanders would hear the passengers' desperate cries and send a rescue boat.

During one momentary break in the waves, he got a look at Ghalib's face.

"Ghalib's mouth was hanging open, and white froth was coming out. He wasn't breathing. His eyes were open, but they were like glass. I was frantic, trying to see Alan's face too."

Each time Abdullah was able to get Alan's head above the water, the boy made no sound. His body was limp, his head lolling to the side. And his eyes were blank, staring. Abdullah thought that if he had a chance to do CPR, he might be able to bring Alan back from the dead. But it was impossible to do anything in that water.

"I held on to the boys for as long as I could, trying to keep their heads above the water. I could not bear to let them go. But I was no match for those waves. One after the other, Ghalib and Alan slipped from my grasp. It was like the sea opened its mouth and swallowed them. راح كل شي, *Rah kilshi*. Everything was gone. I went crazy, thinking, 'I just want to die so that we can be together again.'"

Abdullah gave up the fight and let himself sink under the water. He didn't move his arms or legs. He just wanted to sink to the bottom of the sea and drown. But he kept bobbing back up to the surface.

"I thought, 'They're so light. If I float, maybe they'll float too.' I swam around in circles, frantically calling their names. But no one came to the surface. I was all alone." It was still dark, even with the moonlight. At some point, a searchlight found him in the ink-black sea. It was the coast guard. A helicopter also appeared. As it cast its spotlight on Abdullah, he looked around hopefully for his family—for anyone. When the coast guard ship got to Abdullah, the Iraqi man who had been on his boat reached into the water and pulled him out of that sea.

"*Marti, awladi.* My wife, my kids!" Abdullah yelled. He noticed a man holding a searchlight, and so he grabbed it and went to the edge of the boat, hunching down and casting light across the black water. He couldn't find them, but he couldn't stop calling out to them. The boat and the helicopter searched the waters until daylight. But then the boat began to turn back to the shore.

"Keep circling!" yelled Abdullah. But the coast guard told him they needed to get back to the shore.

"I said to myself, '*Inshallah,* they're going to be waiting at the dock.' " The shock and trauma had split his mind in two, and when he saw the ambulances lined up along the street, his hope turned to dread.

"As soon as my feet hit that dock, I lost it. I became hysterical, hitting myself. I tore at my chest and my T-shirt ripped apart. I started running down the dock, crying their names. I got near one of the ambulances and saw an Iraqi couple from the boat. 'Did you find your family?' 'No.' They said, 'Come to the hospital.' But I couldn't leave the shore. I wanted to look for my family. I went into the coast guard station, but the police said, 'You need treatment. We'll take you to the hospital.' 'I'm not leaving without my family,' I told them. I was crazy, sobbing. After maybe an hour, I convinced myself that they were alive at the hospital and that I had to get there."

A police officer drove Abdullah. En route, the officer stopped to pick someone up. "I think he was a mullah or a sharia lawyer," Abdullah said, "but he was speaking Turkish to the policeman. I thought I heard him say, 'Rest in peace.' I lost all hope. But then I said, 'No, no, no. They're still alive.'"

When they got to the hospital, Abdullah didn't want to go inside. He sat outside on a bench for a while, crying and pulling at his hair. Someone from the hospital eventually came out and took him in. A police officer asked him some questions about the names of the smugglers.

"Where did you leave from?" he asked Abdullah.

"When I told them where we'd left from, he said, 'That's right across the street from the police station. Nobody goes from there.'"

Abdullah was asked to identify the bodies, and then later, he was given one more chance to see them after the autopsy.

"That last look at them will scar my heart forever and ever," Abdullah said.

They lay in front of him, too white and covered in bruises and scratches. They had stitches from being autopsied. By then it was the middle of the night. Afterward, Abdullah was given the bag of his family's clothes and told to go get some sleep, as if he could ever do such a thing.

"I was walking down the same streets we had walked down together, but now I was alone. I called out, 'Where are you, Rehanna? Ghalib? Alan?' I asked God, 'Is it just a bad dream? Please let me wake up from this nightmare.'"

I left Abdullah on October 9, 2015. At the airport, for the thousandth time, I said, "I'm so sorry. How can I leave you like this?"

"You have your family, Fatima. That's all that matters in this life," he responded.

Soon after I left Erbil, Abdullah returned to Kobani for the traditional memorial, forty days after the funeral. Then he decided to go back to Kurdistan to try to continue helping the refugee children in the camps. Before leaving Kobani, though, he packed some of the boys' clothes and favourite toys, as well as a few of Rehanna's possessions—her favourite scarf and dress—and something else that I had no clue he still owned: from the closet of that war-torn bedroom, he removed a dusty suitcase. It was the suitcase filled with baby clothes for Ghalib, which I had brought to Damascus in 2011. When Ghalib no longer needed those baby clothes, Rehanna and Abdullah had lovingly packed them into a suitcase that they'd placed at the back of the closet with the hope of more babies in the future, ideally when the war was over. There's nothing exceptional about saving a baby's possessions for a potential future sibling or for their sentimental value. I still have some of my son's baby clothes that I kept with the hope that I would get to have another child someday. And when I couldn't, I kept them as mementos, for myself, and perhaps for my son and his future children.

Of what use was that suitcase of baby clothes to Abdullah, a man who'd become a solitary ghost haunting a hotel in Erbil? The same use as a few toys and stuffed animals and a woman's scarf and dress; they were the only things that still smelled like his family.

Chapter 13

صاروا طيور

Saaroo toyoor

They Are like Birds Now

On October 13, just a few days after I arrived home from Erbil, I received a phone call from a woman at the Canadian Ministry of Citizenship and Immigration.

"We want you to resubmit your application. We're going to reconsider your private sponsorship for your brother Mohammad and his family," she said.

I couldn't believe it. I cried, out of relief for Mohammad but also out of grief. Why couldn't Rehanna, Ghalib, and Alan be here too?

"Mohammad has another child now," I told her. The woman didn't seem concerned, except she said that the sponsorship of seven people would now cost $35,000. She also needed a photograph of baby Sherwan. It didn't need to be a special passport-style photo, the way it had when I was first applying for asylum for my family. Any photo of the baby would do.

I went to the study to get the application package for Mohammad's family that had been returned to us only four months before, though it seemed as though years had passed. As I looked through the stack of paperwork, I found the unsent papers for Abdullah's family: three copies with three matching sets of photographs of Alan, Ghalib, Rehanna, and Abdullah; and the last page of the application, signed by Abdullah's hand, dated April 14, 2015.

I was crushed. Then I became bitter. I felt once again that we were pawns in a political game. Canadians were gearing up for the federal election, preparing to cast their votes for the country's prime minister. The sudden move to approve my family's application seemed too coincidental. The news that my brother and his family were going to come to Canada made headlines. Before I even knew that the family's resettlement was official, media once again descended on my house for my comments.

"It's too late for Abdullah's family," I told the media, "but hopefully not for many other refugees."

The naysayers were quick to react, saying that it was unfair that Mohammad's family got special treatment, even though Rocco and I were paying for the sponsorship. Some people also thought that since the tragedy, my entire family had been granted special privileges. The truth was that we were just like millions of other desperate refugee families, waiting and hoping for an end to the war that had torn us apart. My own family members were seeds in the wind, scattered across the map. Abdullah was in Kurdistan. In Sham, Baba, Shireen, and two of her kids were about to face their fifth war-ravaged winter. Shireen's son Yasser was still alone in a shelter for children in southern Germany. Mohammad was in another shelter in the distant southern region of Germany, counting the days until his reunion with his family.

196

Back in Turkey, my sister Maha was still in Izmit, two hours from Istanbul; her son Adnan was the only one working, his pay going to the family's rent and living expenses, while I continued to send her money. Hivron was still in Istanbul, but she was barely able to stay afloat. She had been separated from her eldest daughter for more than two years. She and her four youngest kids hadn't seen her husband, Ahmad, since he'd made the crossing and reached Germany two months earlier. Hivron knew it would still be many more months before the German government granted asylum to her and the kids. With Ghouson and her kids preparing for their legal crossing to Canada, Hivron would soon be all alone in Istanbul. She had spent an entire lifetime as the baby sister, always racing to catch up with the rest of us. This situation was no different. She needed to get her family out of Istanbul.

The weather had started to cool. Autumn had arrived and winter was on its heels: the world continued to spin around and around. For refugees, the tick-tock of passing time is magnified. Though Hivron had recently sworn to me that she would never attempt the Mediterranean crossing again, her mind changed a little more with each passing day. "Another hour is upon you," she thought, "and you're still here. Your situation just keeps getting more desperate."

Hivron decided to make her move. She packed whatever she could fit in a knapsack and left Istanbul with her four children. They travelled hundreds of kilometres to Izmir, then undertook a near-disastrous journey by boat across the Mediterranean. Their journey through Europe was fraught with more challenges and danger: at one point, they had to travel on the back of a garbage truck for hours. They reunited with Ahmad in Germany, but Hivron had lost all their IDs, so she could not immediately prove that Ahmad was her husband and the children's father. It would take many weeks of jumping through bureaucratic hoops before they were even allowed to live in the same camp.

While Hivron was making her escape and crossing from one world to the next, the political climate in Canada was heating up. On October 19, 2015, the Liberal Party, under its leader Justin Trudeau, won the election, getting almost 1.5 million more votes than former Conservative prime minister Stephen Harper. Even though Trudeau had made the refugee crisis central to his election campaign, I was worried that the transition would delay the asylum process. But when the reins of power changed hands, Prime Minister Trudeau held to his promise of bringing twenty-five thousand Syrian refugees to Canada.

Shortly after Trudeau's government took power, the new immigration minister, John McCallum, called me to express his condolences.

"When Abdullah is ready to come to Canada," he said, "don't hesitate to contact my office."

With only a few months to prepare for the arrival of Mohammad's family, I did some renovations in our basement to accommodate their family of seven, turning it into a two-bedroom apartment with all the amenities. My neighbour volunteered to do the construction, and a Turkish client of mine did the electric work; both men insisted on working for free. Then we bought mattresses, furnishings, clothes, and some toys for the younger kids. We wanted it to be not just a place for them to stay but a new home.

At the same time, I prepared my new salon, which I called Kurdi Hair Design. I had put that dream on hold after the tragedy, but now that Mohammad was on the way, I pictured us working together there. Maybe one day I would be able to convince Abdullah to apply for asylum too, so that the three of us could work together under one roof. Those optimistic thoughts gave me some hope, but my mourning continued. When I returned from Erbil, I discovered that there were only three molly fish in my tank. I had neglected the fish since the tragedy, and many had died before I left for Europe. After I left, they kept dying, one by one, even though Rocco did his best to care for them. Maybe I was crazy, but I was sure the remaining three fish were the original namesakes of Ghalib, Alan, and Rehanna. One of the fish was larger than the others, so I called her Rehanna.

"I will not let you die," I told those three fish. They were the only living beings that I was equipped to take care of. It was as if I had returned to an infant state. Depression and anxiety closed around me in a tight swaddle. I couldn't eat or sleep. I didn't want to talk to anyone. I tried to go shopping once, just before Mohammad's family arrived. But going outside terrified me. The sky was too big and wide and somehow hostile, especially when it was so arrogantly blue. When I got to the grocery store, I just walked down the aisles, confused and even disgusted by all the choices. I came home with nothing.

At the same time, my old habits continued, as did the schedule I had adopted when Abdullah's family left Istanbul to make the crossing. Every day, I woke up far too early, my heart pounding in my chest. I still rushed to the kitchen to check my cellphone as if the past months had been a terrible dream and my phone might ring to tell me they'd all arrived safe on the other side.

Since returning from Erbil, I called Abdullah every single morning. Our conversations were brief.

"How are you?"

"I'm alive."

"What are you doing?"

"دخان وشاي, *Dikhan w shai*. Smoking and drinking tea."

"What are your plans for the day?"

"I don't know."

When I had any energy at all, it was fueled by bitterness and rage.

I directed it mostly at the world's power brokers. They had gone to the UN in Vienna to sit down at the table and attempt to negotiate peace in Syria. But those global leaders couldn't agree on a peace treaty, and the war continued to rage across Syria as ISIS and the terrorist groups took an increasingly tighter grip on the rebel-held regions.

Worse, people's fear of refugees seemed to be growing, alongside accusations that they were terrorists. I was again in the news, telling the good-hearted people around the world that refugees were peaceful people, that they were victims of war, that they were not terrorists, that they were trying to flee violence and terrorism.

I was nervous for Mohammad's family's arrival. I wanted them to feel safe and welcome. The government arranged for Ghouson and the kids to fly to Germany to reunite with Mohammad after more than six months of separation. The family arrived together in Vancouver on December 28, 2015. The media was at the airport to capture their arrival and broadcast our reunion. The family emerged from customs, carrying Canadian flags and teddy bears that a government official had given them. I must have hugged and kissed my nieces and nephews a hundred times, and I took baby Sherwan into my arms, holding him up so I could show him to the world to ask them, "Look, is this innocent Muslim baby a terrorist?" Once again, we were left to wonder where everyone had been when our family was most in need.

A reporter asked me, "Is this the happy ending you wanted?"

"No, this is not the end. This is the beginning," I said. "I've walked through the tunnel to the end, but I have not found the light yet. I will keep walking until I find that light. I will keep telling the refugees to keep walking—to never give up."

Rocco, Alan, and I had come to the airport in two cars. I took Ghouson, baby Sherwan, and the teenagers, Heveen and Shergo, in my car. During the entire hour-long drive to our home in Coquitlam, Ghouson and the kids kept saying, "Wow, it's so green and clean and peaceful here. Are we dreaming? Are we really in Canada?"

We couldn't wait until we got home so we could call Abdullah.

"I watched their arrival on the news here," he said. "I was crying. It was very emotional. حمد الله على السلامة, *Hamdillah 'ala as-salameh*. Thank God they arrived safely."

"Our hearts are crying for you right now," we responded. "We wish you would come too."

"I need to be close to my family," he responded.

Our friends were waiting for us at home with a banquet of foods, including some Middle Eastern dishes. But the kids would only eat their mom's cooking. I understood. It's the only thing I had wanted when I transplanted to Canada almost twenty-five years before; even Syrian food in a restaurant didn't taste quite right. If I felt that way, imagine what الغربة, *al ghorbah*, was like for my family since they'd fled Syria. They were still reeling from the trauma of the war, the grisly things they had experienced—from the violence that Shergo had to witness in Sham, to the torture by terrorists, to the scary border crossing (which had left a permanent scar on Rezan's arm), to the chronic torment of the refugee life, and the many months of separation after Mohammad reached the German camps.

All the kids adored their uncle Abdullah, their aunt Rehanna, and their young cousins. "Auntie, we loved it when Uncle Abdullah came to visit us. He was so fun and he always made us laugh," Heveen said. They had grown very close to Rehanna, Ghalib, and Alan during their time of refuge in Kobani and Istanbul.

"Auntie, every day I wake up and the first thing I think about is Ghalib and Alan," said ten-year-old Ranim. "I think, 'Maybe it was a bad dream.'"

All my nieces and nephews felt the same way: one day, their cousins were there, and the next day, they had vanished. What can you say to that? "صاروا طيور, *Saaroo toyoor.* They are like birds now," I told them. "They are flying free."

In the early days after my family arrived, they were my only joy, especially baby Sherwan, a lovely boy, just like Alan. I was so happy to have my nieces and nephews here in Canada, but it hurt so much to think about Alan and Ghalib. Whenever we had talked or Skyped, I used to tell Ghalib, "*Inshallah*, when you come to Canada, I will buy you everything you like."

I still woke up early every morning. But now, instead of my spending entire mornings alone with only my three fish for company, Ghouson and the kids would eventually emerge from the basement to have breakfast with me. Baby Sherwan's smile brought me back to the living.

"صباح الخير, *Sabah alkheir.* Good morning, sunshine," I would say, and give his chubby cheeks lots of kisses.

"What does it mean, 'sunshine'?" the kids asked.

"It means the warmth of the sun. It means family."

All I wanted to do was to sit and play with that baby, but there was too much to do. The kids needed new clothes, school supplies, and always groceries. And for the new salon, opening on January 2, I had to plan an open house. When I took the kids shopping, many people recognized them from all the media coverage. "Welcome to Canada," they would say. A few times, people even offered to pay our grocery store bills, which in some cases were as high as three hundred dollars. One day, my wonderful neighbour took the kids to the mall to buy shoes. At one store, two ladies who knew my family's story gave them a fifty-dollar gift card.

The kids started school a month later. The young ones went right into regular classes at the local elementary school; Heveen and Shergo were put in a special class at the local high school, along with about eight other Syrian refugees. Each school put up banners in Arabic saying, "أهلاً وسهلا, *Ahla wa sahla*—Welcome." Many of my friends and clients were wonderfully kind and helpful. Three of them—Kim, Marie, and Helen—provided English classes for the whole family during the weekends and in the evenings. Another one of my neighbours would come over and read to the kids. And whenever the family needed anything, Kitt graciously took them to the grocery store; they would go straight to the international aisle to try to find ingredients that approximated those from home.

When I opened the new salon, the media came to report on the story. Many other curious locals visited too, some for haircuts, others just for selfies.

"This shop will do very well," I said to Mohammad, as we watched all the people stream in and out of the salon. But within a month, it was just Mohammad and me. The supporters who showed up for the opening never came back as clients. It's very difficult to be a barber—or anyone—starting from scratch in your middle years. Mohammad didn't know anyone, and the salon in the suburbs attracted little pedestrian traffic. I knew that I needed to do all the usual things to promote the business, but my heart and my head were not in the mood.

The honeymoon period ended quickly after that. Mohammad and I went back to our old Tom-and-Jerry ways. He didn't like "Tima's rules." When we came home to eat the dinner that Ghouson had prepared, Mohammad wouldn't eat. He said, "I can't breathe when I sit at your table and eat the food you and your husband paid for. I feel like I'm choking." It pained me deeply to hear my big brother talk like that, but I understood that Mohammad had been through many years of trauma and heartache. Soon after, Mohammad stopped coming to the salon or the dinner table; he spent all his time in the basement. His entire family was stuck in the middle of our fighting, and naturally, they took his side. I didn't know what more to do. Once again, in the dining room, it was just me, Rocco, and Alan, and in the big fish tank nearby, my three molly fish.

I cried to my dad about my troubles with Mohammad.

"The war changes people. Be patient," he advised.

Abdullah was very disappointed too. "I talked to Mohammad," he told me. "I said, 'You're with your whole family in a safe country. You have the whole world. ظفر واحد من ولادك بيسوى العالم, *Difr wahad min wlaadak biyswa al'alam.* One nail of your kid's finger is worth more than the whole world.'"

I hoped there was a way forward for all of us. I just needed a sign to tell me how to find it.

Chapter 14

نحنا ولا حدا

Nihna wala hada

We Are Nobody

Whenever my family talks about the tragedy, we always say, "تنذكر وماتنعاد, *Tinzikir wama tin'aad*. To be remembered, but not to repeat." History is meant to be remembered but not repeated. Unfortunately, history does tend to repeat itself. Wars continue, making more tragedy inevitable. What is it about us that we keep repeating the same mistakes over and over and over? I know I must sound pessimistic, but when tragedy strikes, it's hard to tame the fear that life could become even worse, no matter how much you fight off these dark thoughts.

I remained consumed with worry about Abdullah and also Baba, especially when Shireen finally decided it was time to leave Sham and seek refuge in Turkey. Shireen had asthma, but it was difficult to get refills for her puffer, and the youngest of her three sons had developed the same condition. I worried how they would all fare in Turkey and if they'd be able to find the medications they needed. Shireen couldn't convince her husband, Lowee, to leave his disabled mother, so Shireen and two of her sons—Yasser remained in Germany—left on their own and went straight to Izmit to be near Maha. After Shireen left, Baba had no children or grandchildren within reach. All that was left of his family was his constant companion: that big photograph of Mama.

In mid-June, Mohammad's family moved out of our home and into a townhouse nearby. I lost the daily sunshine of my nieces and nephews, but the family visited occasionally. A month later, Rocco and I celebrated our tenth anniversary. To be honest, the significance of that anniversary didn't even register in my mind until my loving husband came to the salon for a haircut just before closing time and reminded me. We went out for a quiet dinner afterward. I tried to not talk about my family, but that was impossible.

Abdullah remained in Erbil through 2016. The KRG continued to host his stay in a hotel. They wanted to provide him with an apartment, but they were still waiting for the complex to be finished. Abdullah was grateful for the KRG's continued support and hospitality, but the hotel had become a velvet prison. When he visited the refugee camps with a delivery of diapers or school supplies, he always sent me a photo. He was smiling; he looked as close as possible to his old self.

President Barzani was also true to his pledge to help fix Abdullah's teeth. It was a long, slow process. It had started the previous fall, and every few months, Abdullah returned to a dentist in Istanbul who fitted him for implants. The visits were both physically and psychologically traumatizing. He called me from Istanbul after one of his appointments in early July, just a few days before Eid.

"I should be with my family, getting ready for Eid, taking my kids to buy new clothes," Abdullah said. "My heart is bleeding. والله, عم موت ألف مرة باليوم *Wallah 'am mout alf marah bilyoum*. Oh God, I'm dying a thousand times a day. I want my family back."

Abdullah was feeling sick in body and mind, so he decided to have a bath. He drifted off to sleep and had a terrible dream: he was back in that water, trying to save his family from drowning. He started yelling and flailing in the bathtub, so loud that hotel staff came to his door. Two days later, after he returned to Erbil, he called me, saying, "My whole body is so stiff, like wood. I don't know what's happening to me, but I can't move."

"Call someone to come and help you, please. Promise me you'll go see the doctor. I don't think you should be alone," I said.

The next morning, Abdullah didn't return my texts or calls. I panicked as I kept calling him, but the phone just rang and rang. Eventually, a relative of ours answered his phone. Abdullah had severe swelling in his limbs, and our relative had taken him to a local hospital. The doctors didn't know what was wrong with him and they wanted to send him to a hospital in Turkey.

"What does that mean, that they don't know what he has?" I asked.

"All they know is that Abdullah is in very bad condition. They are flying him to a hospital in Istanbul now."

I immediately called my sisters. Maha let out a scream when I told her. "He just left. Why would he return here? What's wrong?"

"I don't know," I said. "Can you or Shireen go to the hospital to be with him?"

Luckily, both Maha and Shireen were able to rush to his bedside. Abdullah was diagnosed with sepsis. He was delirious with fever, so delirious he could barely talk, and my sisters couldn't understand him even when he did. The medical treatments that followed confused them too.

One day the doctors would put tubes all over his body. The next his legs would swell up so much that he couldn't walk anymore. My sisters were afraid.

"Tima, we don't know if Abdullah is going to make it," Maha told me. "I told Shireen not to tell Baba. He can't know how bad it is."

"*Inshallah*, he will be okay," I said.

Abdullah was a difficult patient. He would often tell his sisters and the nurses that he didn't want to live, that he just wanted to be with his family. He was attached to his cellphone day and night, constantly watching his collection of videos of his wife and sons. He had lost many photos and images of them when the sea had taken his phone. But many of us also had copies, and while he was at the hotel in Erbil, he had tracked down the majority of lost photos and put them on his new phone, which he guarded closely, clinging to it like a life preserver.

One morning, my cellphone started to chatter. It was a text from Maha. I called her, and while she updated me, I could hear the now-familiar beep of Abdullah's heart monitor in the background. It was too fast.

Along with the havoc of the sepsis on his body, Abdullah's mind was consumed by the pain of the approaching anniversary of the tragedy. The boy that had always been so easygoing, the first to forgive, to turn his cheek, had become withdrawn, untrusting, and uncooperative.

Maha told me Abdullah kept bugging her to take him outside for a cigarette, but the problem was more than that: the doctors also wanted to put a tube down his throat to investigate what was going on in his heart. The very thought of that procedure so filled Abdullah with anxiety, that he would vomit or choke.

"He feels lost, so he's like a kid bugging you for candy," she said. "But the nurses keep telling him that if he smokes, they won't give him the operation he needs; they'll kick him out on the street." I could hear Abdullah grumbling in the background.

I wanted to be brave. "Let me talk to him," I said.

"*Habibi*, please," I begged him. "You need to listen to the nurses."

"So what? I don't care," he responded. "I'm not going to do the surgery anyway. I don't want it."

"Do it for Rehanna and the boys," I said. "So that you can make it to the anniversary." The memorial, which was in Kurdistan, was less than a month away. It was the wrong thing to say. His heart monitor started to beat even faster. It filled me with guilt, a feeling that had become all too familiar since the tragedy.

My sister took the phone back and told me that Abdullah needed to rest. She sounded exhausted from her vigil. Just before she hung up, I heard him in the background saying to her, "Sister, don't leave me alone."

The next day, after more than two weeks in the hospital, Maha arrived to find Abdullah, as always, glued to his phone and crying. She was so worried that this habit was doing him more harm than good that she tried to take his phone away. When they got into a tug-of-war over it, the phone fell on the ground and broke.

"My whole life is on that phone!" he cried. "Maha, go fix it." So Maha, an exhausted, broke refugee, hit the unfamiliar streets of Istanbul and tried to find a place to repair the phone. She was weak from not eating and from many sleepless nights of vigil, and after finally finding a repair shop, as she was walking back to the hospital, she fainted. Luckily, she was close to the hospital. A nurse saw it happen and came rushing out. She took Maha to the hospital lab for blood tests. Maha was okay, just weak from stress and lack of food.

"يا حرام بيحرق القلب, *Ya haram bihriq al-alb.* It will make your heart burn," Maha told me. "Even the nurses feel sorry for him. After all that he went through, they understand, and they try their best to help him."

I was so grateful that my sisters could be there with Abdullah. I wanted so badly to be with my family. But I had a salon to run, and I hoped to be in Erbil with Abdullah for the anniversary of the tragedy. I had to believe he would survive this illness and be back in Kurdistan before September 2.

In early August 2016, with the anniversary of the tragedy just weeks away, the media started calling me again to do follow-up articles about Abdullah and my family. They asked the same question: one year after the tragedy, had the picture of the boy on the beach helped the world understand the refugee crisis? I didn't want to tell the media about Abdullah's health issues. And he was in no shape to do interviews. But with every passing day, it got more and more difficult to hold off the queries of so many reporters. Meanwhile, Abdullah was unlike himself, fluctuating from weak and vulnerable to hostile.

"You're not putting a camera and a big tube down my throat. I will choke and throw up. You need to understand that I don't care if I'll die," he would bark at the nurses.

"We have to do this procedure to prepare for your surgery," the nurses would respond.

"I'm not having surgery."

"It's the only thing we can do to save your life."

"I don't care about my life."

Maha and Shireen shy away from conflict, so it was my job to talk to Abdullah.

"Baba is worried about you," I told Abdullah on the phone. "He wants you to live and move on. We all do: we can't take more pain. We need you to listen to the doctors and have the treatments that will help you get better, please."

Abdullah said something in reply, but I couldn't understand it; he was still having difficulty speaking. Shireen took the phone back. "We can only pray to God for help," she said.

Finally, after many days of arguing and lashing out, Abdullah agreed to have the scope procedure. After that, he was scheduled for surgery to clear the fluids and toxins from his heart and chest.

"I think the doctors are finally getting through to him," Maha said. "But before the surgery Abdullah needs a blood transfusion. Luckily, some people from the KRG are here to help. They found a blood donor," said Maha. "Today, he called me and Shireen to sit on his bed. Then he hugged us so hard, and whispered, 'Forgive me for this. Thank you for helping me.'"

Before Abdullah had the surgery, we all talked to him on the phone.

"Please forgive me if I don't make it," he said to me. "If I don't, I want you to continue to put your voice out there. Someone has to keep speaking for these innocent people."

"Don't talk like that. *Allah karim*," I said. "You'll be the one who goes out there to help them. You'll be fine."

Thankfully, he was. After ten more days of antibiotics and recovery, Abdullah was mostly recovered from the sepsis. And then, a month after he entered the hospital with this horrible life threat, Abdullah did something he hadn't done since the tragedy: he sent us all a silly video. For the first time in almost a year, we allowed ourselves to say, "Abdullah is finally back."

But more challenges lay ahead. Abdullah would soon have to face the anniversary of the tragedy. He was released from the hospital in mid-August, and he returned to Kurdistan soon after. The KRG was planning a memorial service for Adbullah's wife and children.

"I don't want to be alone for the anniversary. Can you come to Erbil?" he asked me.

I told him I'd try my best. I was desperate to see him again, and so I put everything on hold to get to Kurdistan to be with him. It had been a year since I last saw Abdullah, and it was even more heartbreaking to see him this time. He was skinny and pale; his vocal cords had been injured during the operation, and he could barely walk or even talk. Thankfully, Abdullah now had a home to go to. The government generously provided him with a furnished townhouse, which was a great relief. Before my arrival, he had moved in many of his personal possessions, but he had not yet slept there. We stopped off at the hotel to gather the last of his things.

At the townhouse, I put my luggage in the guest room and freshened up. Then I explored the house. I stopped cold in my tracks when I got to Abdullah's bedroom. His bed was covered with his kids' stuffed animals. And there were more of their toys in a cabinet. Abdullah came in, opened the closet, and pulled out the suitcase filled with the kids' old baby clothes, the one I had brought to Sham in 2011. Abdullah opened a cabinet drawer and placed the baby clothes in it, one piece at a time.

"Remember these?" he said, holding up a pair of baby shoes. "And this toy?" He picked up the Sesame Street doll I'd seen him holding on the news. He held the toy to his face, breathed deeply, and started to cry.

"ريحتن راحت, *Reehton rahit.* Their smell is gone," he sobbed. "The suitcase was full of dust, so I got the clothes washed at the hotel. Why did I do that?"

"Please, Abdullah, stop it. Don't torture yourself," I said. Then I tried to comfort him, saying, "Maybe someday you will get married again and have more kids." It was the wrong thing to say.

"How am I going to find another woman like Rehanna?" he asked. "She was the perfect wife and a loving mother."

It hurt me to watch my brother suffering. Even in the safety of his new house, Abdullah was still in constant pain from the surgery and the tragedy. We were all alone, and I considered what a strange place we were in. I realized that there were no hospitals or medical clinics nearby to provide the follow-up medical care that he needed, and I wondered what my brother would do if something happened to him when he was alone. That night, in the guest bedroom, I stared at the crisp white ceiling for a long time, thinking about the past and wondering, *What's next? How can I help him?*

The world isn't fair, I thought, as I cried myself to sleep.

I don't know how Abdullah managed to stay alive for a whole year all by himself. He was slowly healing, but he now had many scars on the outside, to match the ones inside, from his surgery. The incision stretched from his trachea to his belly button, and beneath that there were three smaller incisions where tubes had been inserted to reach his other vital organs. His dental work remained unfinished, so he still couldn't chew food. On the morning of the memorial, we went shopping for yogurt and lots of fruit to make smoothies. When we got to the counter, Abdullah held up some Bubblicious gum.

"Smell it," he said. "It still smells just like it did when we were kids. It reminds me of all the holiday parties back in Sham. Remember Mama would be cooking all day, and she'd send us down to the store, and we'd buy this gum for one franc?"

"And she'd say, 'حبيبي, *Habibi*, don't stop and play with your friends. I need that parsley and eggplant.'"

"Remember the mess after those parties? Everybody yelling, 'You do the dishes. You wash the floor.' We didn't go to sleep until four a.m."

Now grief and worry and nightmares kept us up all night. Now we found ourselves rushing back to the townhouse to do media interviews.

Abdullah wanted to repeat his message: stop the war, let the Syrian people go home, and in the meantime, help the refugees. There were many outlets clamouring for exclusive interviews, but Abdullah agreed to do only a few, with the German paper *Bild*, BBC TV, and some Arabic media. After seeing his condition, I knew that he had to save all his strength for the memorial service. The media would have to make do with talking to me. My email and cellphone didn't stop pinging from the moment I arrived in Erbil. I did a number of Facetime interviews and a live interview with ITV on the morning of the anniversary for their UK breakfast TV show. I also did interviews with CNN, Sky Media, and many newspapers and radio stations from all over the world.

That night, we went to the memorial. The Kurdish people put on a beautiful service at the refugee camp. The refugees had made a feature-length movie dramatizing the story of my brother's family's tragedy and that of the Kurdish people. The movie was beautiful but also so heartbreaking that Abdullah and I cried from start to finish. When we returned to the townhouse, Abdullah retreated to his bedroom. In the middle of the night, I woke up to the sound of him yelling, "Alan! Ghalib! Rehanna!" I jumped out of my bed and rushed to his room. He was sitting upright in bed, but he appeared to be asleep.

"What's wrong?" I asked, grasping Abdullah's shoulder.

"I have pains in my chest," he said. Then, after a few moments, "I had a dream I was with my family."

I couldn't go back to sleep. It was three a.m. I went downstairs and made some coffee. I opened the front door and sat for a few hours, smoking, drinking coffee, and thinking about my family until it felt as if my heart would burst. I looked up to the sky and started praying to God to heal Abdullah. I even asked Alan and Ghalib and Mama in heaven for help. My chest was burning and tears poured down my face. Then, as the sun began to rise, two birds appeared. They danced and chirped in the air above me. One was bigger than the other.

"Ghalib? Alan?" I said out loud. Then, to myself, "You're crazy, Tima." But those birds continued to dance and sing until my tears stopped.

A little while later, for the first time since my arrival, Abdullah came downstairs to have breakfast with me. It seemed like another good sign, and my heart was finally happy.

Thank you, God, Mama, Ghalib, and Alan, I thought.

There was still a long road ahead, though. Abdullah's nightmares continued for the next few days. I did some research on local medical organizations that might be able to treat both Abdullah's physical and psychological wounds. I found two clinics online that specialized in post–traumatic stress disorder for victims of war. But when I contacted the clinics, they said that they didn't have the resources to deal with new patients. And even if they had, Abdullah still didn't want to see a doctor, let alone get help for his ailing mind. All sorts of things in the waking world triggered Abdullah's trauma and grief. One morning, while I was cleaning the counters, Abdullah came down for breakfast, breathed deeply, and said, "*Ah, ya Allah, ekhti*, that was Rehanna's favourite cleaner."

I wanted so badly to take away his pain and turn his mind to something that would make him feel better. "Why don't we go visit the kids at the refugee camp?" I suggested.

Abdullah brightened at the idea. "We can't go empty-handed. Let's bring diapers for the babies."

"Okay. Is five hundred dollars' worth of diapers enough?"

"Anything is better than nothing."

Abdullah called a grocery store in Erbil, put in an order for five hundred dollars' worth of diapers, and then called the camp supervisor to arrange our visit. We picked the diapers up the next day and drove straight to the camp. When we got there, word spread quickly, and within minutes, hundreds of refugees flocked to the camp entrance, so many people that we had to tell them to go back to their homes and that we'd come around to deliver the diapers to families that needed them. As we walked around looking for families with babies, many refugees invited us to share a meal with them. It was so typical of Syrian and Kurdish hospitality: even though they didn't have enough food for themselves, they wanted to share their last piece of bread with us. It reminded me so much of home. We talked to many of them, and each one had his or her own painful story. I saw the suffering in their eyes, felt the pain in their hearts. Everyone was desperate to go back home to Syria. I kept looking at Abdullah as we shook our heads in sympathy, and after listening to their stories, we would say, "لا حول ولا قوة إلّا بالله, *La hawl w la qowwata illa billah.* There is no strength without God."

Abdullah only lit up around kids. We didn't have enough diapers for all those needy people, so we promised to return soon. After we left the camp, we drove to the top of a nearby hill that overlooked it and sat to catch our breath. I told myself that one day, he might be healthy enough to remarry and have more children. But Abdullah's mind was elsewhere.

"Look at all these families," he said, staring down at the camp. "Then imagine all the millions of other families living in camps, getting so desperate that they risk that crossing. I don't know if I can stand hearing more stories about people drowning in that sea. It's not fair. All these charities spending billions of dollars in aid, and it's still not enough. I want to do it myself. And deliver it myself, so I can ask, 'What else do you need?'"

"It will be impossible to help everyone."

"At least we can try. I thought that photo of Alan was the true wake-up call. A year later, did everybody forget? If this war doesn't stop, there will be more starvation, more suffering. We need to end this war."

"Who are *we*? We can't even help our families," I said. "We are nobody."

When Rocco picked me up at the airport in Vancouver, I'm ashamed to say that the first thing out of my mouth was, "I didn't want to leave. I don't want to be here." Rocco and Alan deserve sainthood for continuing to love and support me in so many ways. I returned to life at my salon, working Tuesdays through Saturdays. But the only thing that sparked my imagination was my recent conversations with Abdullah—about starting a charity, about keeping Rehanna, Ghalib, and Alan's voices alive. I started to think, "So what that we are nobodies? Even nobodies have a voice."

We could either wallow in shame and misery or continue to use our voices to stop the war and the refugee crisis. I decided to reach out to high schools and universities. I told them that I was available to talk, to share my family's story in the hopes that it would motivate the students to help others in need. Many schools were happy to host me, and I met many beautiful young adults who wanted to help the refugees in some way or another.

"You don't need to do something big," I would tell them. "Imagine yourself starting in your community, helping your needy neighbours. Even if you plant one seed, keep watering it and that seed will grow into something beautiful."

"Tima, you've given me hope," a student told me after one of my talks. "I want to find a way to sponsor a refugee family and bring them to Canada."

Words like that were so beautiful to hear that they gave me the power to keep speaking. It was worth it. Like my *baba* always said, "Forget what hurts you. It won't change anything. Be proud of yourself and remember that our story is one of many. *Inshallah*, everyone will follow your courage."

I wanted to realize my brother's dream of helping refugees everywhere. So I called Abdullah and said, "Let's start a charity in our family's name, dedicated to Ghalib and Alan and all the refugee kids."

"How do we do that?"

"I have no clue. I can register it here, and we can start by focusing on the kids near you in the Kurdistan-based camps. Then, when it's safe, hopefully we can help the ones in Syria, and if we can make it grow, we can start helping other children and refugees around the world."

"Fatima, if I could deliver anything to those kids, my life would be worth living."

I called a local lawyer, who offered to help with the legal work for free. It would take six months or even longer for our charity to become registered. I created a basic website for anyone willing to provide support in the meantime. It wasn't much, but it was a start. Finally, we had a way forward.

Chapter 15

الشجرة مرات لا تعيش إذا غيرنا مكانا

Al-shajarah marat la t'eish iza ghyirna makana

Trees Often Transplanted Never Prosper

I'm in Sham, at our family's house, making snowballs with Abdullah and our friends on the rooftop. We are so happy it's snowing. The snow rarely survives a full day. The sun will come out and it will melt, and the steep, cobbled streets will flood and glisten. We want to make the most of every second in the snow. Abdullah races down to the kitchen and returns with a bowl. He makes a snowball and rolls it in the bowl until it glitters.

"I made something special for you," he says. "Have a seat, and enjoy my *hab al-'aziz*." He hands me a snowball coated in anise seed and sugar.

"Mom!" someone calls out, startling me out of my daydream.

I was not a child in Sham anymore. I was standing at my kitchen window, staring out at the falling snow. It was December 2016. My son,

Alan, was standing behind me, saying, "I'm going to shovel the driveway so that you can get your car out later."

"Okay, thanks."

"Then I'm going to work."

I should have said, "Put on a hat and gloves," but I didn't. Alan was already an adult. He could take care of himself. He didn't need me. But I knew that was only half the truth. We always need our mothers.

With Christmas just around the corner, I could have been baking my son's favourite cookies and shopping for gifts for my family. But I had other duties that day. Prime Minister Justin Trudeau was visiting Vancouver, and the local media had planned a small town-hall-style meeting. I was invited to participate and ask him a question related to Syria.

When my time to pose a question arrived, I stood and addressed the prime minister.

"Thank you for bringing more than thirty thousand refugees to Canada and saving their lives," I said. "But there are still millions of refugees suffering around the world who need our help. What can Canada do to help find a political solution to end the war in Syria?"

"Don't thank me," Trudeau said. "Thank the many Canadians who helped sponsor and support the refugees. There are millions of refugees who still need help, and I wish Canada could accept them all. But we just can't help everyone."

I waited for Trudeau to continue explaining. I hoped he would tell us how Canada was doing its best, or how it was planning to take in more refugees. But instead, the town hall moved on to the next question. I sat back down, confused and disappointed.

Afterward, Trudeau shook hands with everyone in attendance. When it was my turn, I stretched out my hand, but he gave me a hug, saying,

"I'm so pleased to meet you. Thank you for what you're doing for refugees." At that moment, Trudeau the politician disappeared and I could see a kind, caring father expressing deep sorrow for my family's tragedy. Then he moved on to shake hands with the next attendee.

A few mornings later, I was at the kitchen window once again, hypnotized by the snow that never seemed to stop and thinking about my family in Turkey and Germany, as well as the poor refugees that I had met in the camps. I worried about how they would survive another cold winter. Alan broke the spell once again.

"I'm graduating today. I'm done," he said. It hit me that since the tragedy, I'd paid almost no attention to my son or my husband. Depression had been running my life, eating away at me. "Wake up, Tima," I told myself. "You're missing so much."

I grabbed Alan and kissed him and hugged him, saying, "I'm so proud of you."

I'd always been incredibly proud of my son. He had always been a considerate and thoughtful soul. When I was a broke, single mom, he never whined for expensive gifts. He loved Lego, but even as a young boy, he understood it was very expensive; if he pooled all his savings, he could buy a small tub of Lego, and that was okay with him; he was always patient and giving. Once, as a little kid, he counted out all the savings in his piggy bank and gave the money to me, saying, "I want to give it to kids in need." I couldn't have asked for a better son than Alan. In return, since the tragedy, or maybe even before that, after my trip to Istanbul in 2014, I'd been a neglectful mother.

I was white-knuckled as I navigated the icy streets to my salon. I'd never learned how to drive in the snow. I thought about turning back, but I told myself, "Just keep moving forward." I had only a few appointments booked. I knew how to promote my business, but I wasn't trying. I had a dozen long-time clients, but otherwise I left things up to chance walk-ins. My salon was losing more money every day, and I was too preoccupied about Abdullah and my family to figure out a business solution, which was a vicious cycle, because every wasted dollar filled me with guilt. A few hours later, a pretty woman entered the salon. She wanted to freshen up her highlights for a big party.

I could pay attention when I was working because I was a professional and because my tools were scissors and bleach. I never forgot that first bleaching job with Lina. I'd been scrupulous and careful ever since. But I didn't love my job anymore. I didn't even understand it. Why did people care so much about superficial things? I had once been like them. Sometimes I wanted that person back. But I couldn't go back. I couldn't forget all the beautiful, brave refugees. I couldn't forget my people. War changes people.

One day that winter, I received a surprising phone call at the salon. It was Chris Alexander, the former immigration minister. Almost two years after I wrote to him, sending many emails begging him to reconsider the restrictions on refugees, he called to say that he was sorry for my family's loss. He wanted to meet me for coffee during an upcoming trip to Vancouver. A few days later, we were sitting across from each other at a table. He brought his cousin, a lawyer, who presented me with a plant wrapped in a pink ribbon. We were discussing the refugee crisis. "People called me a child killer," he said. He said that my family's tragedy caused his party to lose the election.

"I would never call you that or put the blame on you or any single person; I blame us all," I told him. "But I wish you had listened to my letters and that you had done something to change the impossible restrictions for Syrians. Then we would have been able to bring Abdullah's family to Canada."

"I did instruct my office to call and tell you to resubmit Mohammad's family's application," he said.

Alexander went on to say he was now listening and that he wanted to work with me to stop the violence in Syria. I was all ears.

"I don't support violence and I don't take political sides, one way or the other. I'm on the side of the people stuck in the middle," I said. "My message is about peace. About laying down weapons and sitting down at a table to come to a compromise. It's about letting the citizens of Syria return home and decide their own fate."

Our meeting ended after Alexander's cousin took a photograph of the two of us. The exchange left me with a feeling that was all too familiar since the tragedy and my trip to the UN in Brussels: doubt. I had come to doubt that politicians would act on their promises to prevent more senseless deaths. I felt once again like a pawn on a chessboard, with each square a slightly different shade of grey. I'd become less naïve about the fact that millions of people were caught up in a power struggle controlled by the rich and the influential—a struggle causing the sacrifice of many pawns.

It's the poor people who suffer most, at the hands of the powerful, the mighty who pull the strings and the levers. Those puppet masters aren't just oblivious to the suffering of the poor: they create it and line their pockets with it. They step on people's heads and shoulders, pushing them down, crushing them into the ground, ripping their roots from the soil and tossing them into the wind. It's like that everywhere, from Canada to Syria. The poor are always victims of injustice. They are the casualties of war.

Shortly after my meeting with Alexander, the United States became caught up in the controversy of the so-called Muslim ban. I was deeply upset when I first heard the details. It brought to mind an old Arabic expression about hypocrisy: "نقتل القتيل ونمشي في جنازته". We killed the person, but we mourn at their funeral."

A few weeks later, I found myself in Washington, DC. American congresswoman Tulsi Gabbard had invited me to be her guest at President Trump's inaugural congressional address on February 28. My instincts told me that Tulsi had a beautiful soul and that we shared the desire for a peaceful end to the Syrian war. Her message to the American people was simple: Stop arming the Syrian rebels with weapons, because those weapons have too often fallen into the hands of terrorists, causing the death and displacement of innocent Syrians caught in the middle.

My seat at Trump's address to Congress was on the balcony level, directly across from Trump. I'll admit that I didn't pay much attention to what he was saying; I doubted he would address the war in Syria. When it did come up, all he said was that he would defeat ISIS. The following day, I did many interviews with the media. It seemed the whole world wanted me to pick a side, but I delivered the same message I'd been repeating since the first day after the tragedy: end the war in Syria; stop pointing fingers; help those caught in the middle. Because I was in America, a country that has taken in so few Syrian refugees, I also said that if the United States stopped bombing my country, the Syrian people wouldn't have to come to America. To finish my trip, I did a talk at George Washington University. I loved the lively discussion with the students most of all. They were earnest and thoughtful, eager to do something to effect change, but they admitted they felt overwhelmed about how to go about doing it.

"I want to help financially, but I don't have much money," said one young woman. I told her that even if she set aside a dollar every week, by the end of the year, she'd have enough money to help a refugee family in Turkey.

I returned home to find that, after the comments I'd made, some people had made death threats against me. I had grown somewhat accustomed to attacks from critics filling the comments sections of online news feeds with nasty comments about me and Abdullah. Yet these new rants were even worse than usual. These detractors felt I didn't have a right to voice my opposition to the arming of rebels or *anyone* who took up arms and inflicted violence upon innocent civilians. Some critics told me to shut my mouth, that I had no right to voice any opinion at all because I was a woman. How dare I call for a peaceful solution to end this war?

I was shocked and heartbroken to hear those hateful words, some of them from my own Syrian people. Their sentiments were in stark contrast to the Syrian belief I grew up with—the belief in living side by side in peace and tolerance. Did the war do this to my people? These attacks made me consider backing out of the spotlight. But once again, Rocco and Alan lifted me up.

"You can't pay attention to the haters," said Alan. "You can't give up, that's what they want. You can't let them win. You should be proud of yourself. Your voice helped bring so many people to Canada and countries all over the world."

I took my son's advice. But how do you win when hate has weapons of modern warfare on its side?

I realized that I needed to commit myself completely to advocacy. I decided to close my hair salon. I found someone to whom I could sublease it. My final day was March 29, 2017. It was sad to lock the door for the last time, but people have a lot of dreams that don't always work out. And my heart was never in it, because it happened at the wrong time. My only thoughts now were about how I could help refugees and use my voice to try to stop the war.

The following day, I flew to Ontario to do a talk at the University of

Waterloo. Soon after, I went to Philadelphia to give a speech at Temple University. It was still hard for me to talk about what my family had been through, but it was heartening to bring awareness to young people, and I found that being around young adults was very inspiring. They were often shocked to hear that my siblings were all still living a life of poverty and hardship as refugees in foreign lands.

In early April 2017, Abdullah went back to the dentist in Turkey. His new implants were finally ready. He was about to get them installed when he saw photographs of the chemical attack in Syria—so many innocent children maimed or dead. Abdullah called me in hysterics.

"How on earth can any human being be so evil? How can they harm children and elderly people?" he said. "*Wallah haram*. It is forbidden. How many more shocking images of children does the world need to see before they stop this war?"

That night, I woke up to a terrible sound. My forty-litre fish tank had somehow ruptured, flooding my living room. I rushed to the room and found that my three fish—Rehanna, Ghalib, and Alan—were dead.

Epilogue

Jasmine-Scented Air

It's been six summers since the uprising in Syria began, and my family continues to try to find its place in an ever-changing world. In December 2016, Hivron's family got out of the shelter in Germany. They were granted a year-long asylum, which enabled them to move into a furnished house in a town near the shelter. When they arrived at their new house, the family was greeted with a large basket filled with fruit on the dining room table—a welcome gift from their neighbours. Hivron sent me a video: a tour of her new home. "It makes me hopeful, but it also fills me with *ghorbah*," she said.

Hivron has since made some wonderful friends and allies in that small town. It's the kind of place where everybody knows their neighbours and everyone is friendly, no matter what racial background you come from.

"My neighbours here are just like the ones back home," Hivron said

TIMA KURDI

to me. "Yesterday, my washing machine broke, and my German neighbour took all our laundry and washed it herself."

A few other Syrian families live there as well. They meet once a week at the local church to receive German lessons. Hivron's husband, Ahmad, does workfare jobs for the government. One day he plants flowers in the public gardens, and the next day he does janitorial work, all as part of a practical work training component of his asylum.

"I can't find a job," Hivron says. "And I wonder if we would be better off in a larger city. But my neighbour keeps saying, 'I think your family is safer here.'"

The most important thing is that their kids have been able to enrol in school and her younger children have adapted well to Germany. Eighteen-year-old Abdulrahman found it very tough initially. He was bullied at school by a handful of mean teenagers. "Go back to Syria, you terrorist!" they taunted.

"Auntie, they say we're bad people," he once said when we talked on the phone. "Why don't they understand that we're here because we're peaceful? That we're here to escape violence and war. That we're just looking for a safe place to live?"

It is no wonder that my nephew struggled with school.

"I want to learn a trade and start working and making money," he continued. "I want to be a man and take care of my family."

At the same time, the trauma that he and Shergo suffered in Sham as young boys haunts him. He misses his uncle Abdullah, and he remains heartbroken about the loss of his cousins.

Hivron's most traumatic flashbacks are a result of her many attempted sea crossings. When her German neighbours invited her family to a day at the beach in the North Sea, she happily accepted.

"Fatima, as soon as I was there, I got right back in that sea. I was always such a good swimmer before," she says. "Next thing I knew, I felt like I was drowning. I had a complete meltdown. Everyone must have thought I was a total kook."

Shireen and Maha and their kids remain refugees in Izmit, Turkey. Shireen has her two young sons with her. Farzat isn't in school because he has to work, but Maleek is going and he enjoys it. The Turkish government has recently started providing aid to refugees, making life much easier than it was before. Shireen gets three hundred lira a month to cover her daily expenses, and I'm still helping with her rent. But her husband remains in Sham, and her eldest son, Yasser, is still in a shelter in Heidelberg. As an unaccompanied minor, he receives extra resources, like language classes, and he's also taking acting classes; he recently wrote and performed a play about his life. But whenever he talks to his mama, Yasser tells her how much he misses her and his *baba* and brothers.

Maha's husband recently suffered a stroke that left him unable to speak and paralyzed in one arm and one leg. He couldn't eat for two weeks, and it took more than a month for them to get a wheelchair so that Maha could move him to the bathroom or out to the balcony to get some fresh air. He will need surgery to unblock a vein in his neck, and he will also need intensive rehabilitation to relearn how to speak and regain the use of his limbs. Maha is worried that these health resources will be impossible for him to get in Turkey. Now her eldest son, Adnan, is the only working member of the family, so I still help them financially too. Her daughter Barehan remains in Kurdistan and her son Mahmoud in a German shelter.

Mohammad and his family live around the corner from me in Vancouver. The best news is that the kids are adapting well to life and school. Their eldest daughter, Heveen, plans to become a dentist one day. Both Heveen and Shergo are working part-time. Baby Sherwan's teeth are coming in now. When he turned two, we had a nice party for his birthday.

"How old are you?" I asked him in English, holding up two fingers as a hint.

He responded with baby talk.

I said, "You're two. Tell me how old you are."

It only took a few tries before he said, "Two!"

He was thrilled to blow out the candles on his birthday cake. He loved it so much that he wanted the candles relit ten times, just so he could blow them out again and again. That boy brings me so much joy. When he calls out, "Auntie," it is music to my ears. Such a smiling, happy little boy—I know it isn't fair to him, but every time I see his beautiful, smiling face, I think about Alan.

My father is still in the house at the top of the mountain in Damascus, living with his adopted daughter, Duaa, and her young son, Youssef, two Syrians in need whom my generous father could not turn away. But his heart aches for his own kids and grandkids. Being a grandfather has always given him a lot of joy. The war took that from him. It gives me some comfort to know that Baba still has Duaa and her young son living in the house. Youssef's learning disability is a challenge, but he's loving and innocent, always happy and laughing—a ray of sunshine every day.

Baba and some of my Syrian friends have said that Damascus has been relatively peaceful recently. "The city is bustling again," he says. "I miss you and I want you to come for a visit." Other Syrians are returning to the country no matter what the situation: they'd rather die in their homeland than live and die as poor, starving refugees in a foreign land. I hope that my *baba* is right and that peace is finally taking hold.

Duaa took a photo of Baba recently, sitting on his cushions under the picture of Mama. He looks gaunt and his eyes are sad and wounded. He's our family's precious old treasure, and I pray each day that he will survive, just as millions of others pray that their remaining treasures—their grandparents, their grandkids, their nephews and aunties—will survive to see the end of this war.

Until then, all my refugee siblings continue to dream of returning home, but as time passes, memories of home become foggier. Adaptation is a blessing and a curse. The younger kids in my family barely even recall their country of origin. On the one hand, it's important for kids to adjust healthily to life in their places of refuge, to feel safe, and to feel that they belong in their new communities. On the other hand, they are forgetting their roots. Maybe that's one of the reasons why my siblings and I so often talk about the past.

It's Eid once again, and once again, we are celebrating by living in our memories.

"For the last six years, we've said the same thing every Eid," Hivron observed recently.

"*Inshallah*, next Eid we will finally be together again," we replied in unison.

If the war in Syria ever ends, will my nieces and nephews, along with so many Syrian children, want to go back? Whatever happens, my family will be torn, perhaps even before they have recovered from the trauma of being uprooted in the first place.

We have an Arabic saying: "Trees often transplanted never prosper." I hope that's not true for people. So much depends on the richness of the soil. My nephew Shergo wrote a beautiful poem about his experience of coming to Canada, comparing himself to an uprooted plant. His words are a reminder: everyone, everything, needs soil and water to grow.

In the first six months of 2017, more than eighty thousand refugees risked the Mediterranean crossing; almost two thousand people perished. With each of those deaths, Abdullah's heart breaks a little more.

"The clay pot is shattered into pieces," Abdullah said recently. "How are we going to fix it? Even if we do, there will always be scars. *Inshallah*, the pot can be fixed one day. But how can we sit by and watch people drown in that sea? Why do we keep letting the sea swallow them whole?"

The writing of this book has been a monumental challenge for Abdullah. For the past year, I have nagged him weekly and sometimes daily for details about his life before the tragedy.

"You planted the seed," I remind him. "You said we should write this book."

"My story is no more important than anyone else's."

"But people want to know our family's story. They want to know about Rehanna and Ghalib and Alan. And we want to keep their voices alive. We want to fill the silence left from too many senseless deaths. We want to do what we can to stop the war."

"Fatima, we were just like millions of other refugees."

"Yes, you were. You are. But if you talk about the tragedy that you endured, it might stop more people from drowning in that sea."

"Okay, sister. What I have learned is that it doesn't matter if you have no money and you live in a shed eating lentils. All that matters is that your family is there, that you have love. Love gives us strength and power to forget the suffering and pain. Tell the people. Tell them nothing else matters. We don't thank God enough for all the things we have. We want more and more things. I would trade anything to be with my family again, even in a refugee camp."

That conversation with Abdullah, like so many others, is a revelation to me. It reminds me of an old Arabic proverb: "Children are buttons that hold their parents together." I don't think I realized it at the time, but I know now that when Baba said that war changes people, he wasn't just referring to my brother, he was also referring to me. I realize that since Adbullah's family set out to make the crossing, I've been living in a siege state, hoping for the best, thinking the worst. In many ways, I've put my own family's life on hold. I haven't appreciated them enough. My living nieces and nephews are growing up fast, and I've already missed so much. You can lose everything in the blink of an eye. I need to make the most of my time with all of them. I need to live in the present as much as possible. I'm going to try harder to be the wife and mother and aunt that my family deserves. I'm going to try to be the person that I never got the chance to be for Ghalib and Alan.

I'm not sure if writing this book has helped me find the answers to the many questions that have haunted me since the tragedy. But I hope that by reading my family's story, you will be able to see that we are all essentially the same: we all dream of healthy, peaceful, safe lives for the ones we love. People are more important than money or power. We are more similar than we are different, and we are stronger when united.

With the second anniversary of the tragedy looming, our futures are precarious. All of us are still lost at sea, with no clue where we will end up. But we are alive.

"I hate September. Everything terrible happens in September," my brother Abdullah says. The terrorists invaded Kobani in September, forcing Rehanna and the boys to flee for their lives. The following September, they were dead. That's one of the many reasons why it's still so difficult for my brother and my entire family to look at that photograph of the boy on the beach, of Alan. Many well-intentioned people post that photo, sharing it in the spirit of helping refugees. We are willing to swallow the heartache that photo causes in the hopes that it will prevent more suffering and deaths. But many others help themselves to the photograph to support their own political agendas. We are powerless to stop that because we don't own the photograph of the boy on the beach, yet for Abdullah, it is a literal reminder of the horrible moment when his wife and sons slipped from his grasp.

I don't want Abdullah to be alone for another anniversary. I can't forget my long-ago pledge to my mother: to find Abdullah a wife. It's a promise that my brother might call meddling, but it comes from a place of hope and love.

"We need to find Abdullah a wife," I said to Maha a while back.

"I'll start asking around," she replied. Through the Kobani grapevine, Maha and her friends heard about a woman from Kobani now living as a refugee in Turkey. Ghamzeh is her name. Maha didn't know many details about this woman, but my dad heard about her parents from Kobani; her mom died when she was three years old, just like my *baba*'s had. My dad and sisters convinced Abdullah to meet her during one of his trips to the dentist in Turkey. We said to him, "Life must go on."

After he met Ghamzeh, Abdullah texted me a picture.

"Where did you get this picture of Rehanna?" I asked him.

"It's Ghamzeh."

I could hardly believe it. "She's like Rehanna's twin."

"I know. Her voice is like Rehanna's too."

Both of my sisters liked Ghamzeh instantly. "She's so sweet and down-to-earth," Shireen said. "Even when we call her Rehanna by mistake, she understands."

A few months later, they got married. The night before their small wedding, Abdullah called Maha in a panic, saying, "Why did you push me into this? I can't breathe." He'd just awoken from a dream. Alan had come running into his bedroom and started to dance in a circle, clapping his hands. Rehanna appeared and stood in the doorway, watching Abdullah. Then she smiled, turned her back, and walked away.

"يمكن زعلانين مني, *Yimkin za'lanin minni*. Maybe they are upset?" he wondered. "Maybe they don't want me to get married? شو عملت انا, *Sho 'milt ana?* What have I done, Maha? I can't go through with this."

Maha calmed him down. "It'll take time to adjust. You like Ghamzeh. She likes you. You might fall in love one day."

Abdullah and Ghamzeh were married the next day. Maha and Shireen were there for the ceremony. I hope it works out for those two. I hope that one day, Abdullah will be ready to have more kids.

If Abdullah can survive and still grasp on to hope, I have to tell myself that I can too. Recently I've allowed myself to think that maybe the war can also change us for the better. We can't rewrite history, no matter how much we want to. But we can find a new purpose in life. Before the war, I was an average, middle-class, middle-aged suburban woman—a mother, a wife, and a hairdresser who loved to cook, socialize with friends, and travel to interesting places. When terrible things happened to other people, I empathized with them. But I didn't understand them the way I do now. I would write a cheque to support a charity, donate to food banks, and do all the things that are easy. Then I would go right back to living my life. After the war, and especially after the tragedy, I changed.

I still have no regrets about my crossing to Canada twenty-six years ago. Because I had my son, Alan. Because I met Rocco. Because by living in North America and learning to speak English, I have been able to be the voice for my family and one of the voices of advocacy for the Syrian people. I still find it very strange that the public and the media want me, a nobody hairdresser, to answer the same very big questions that I continue to ask the world. They want to know whether Alan's photograph woke up the world to the plight of the Syrian people. I think it did: I see the millions of people around the world, all the grandparents and parents and aunties and uncles and kids, who continue to say, "Enough is enough," and continue to open their hearts and their doors to needy refugees and victims of war. If I thanked each of them—*each of you*—a thousand times, it wouldn't be enough to convey my gratitude.

But I don't think that photograph of Alan woke up the politicians and heads of state. I think many of those giants are still sleeping. I think their hearts are still blind. I will do my best to keep helping my family and refugees everywhere—to be a voice for the people who can't speak. I am constantly reminded of something that many of them have said to me: "The world is talking *about* us. But no one talks *to* us."

In the hopes that Abdullah and I can continue to talk to refugees—and most importantly, to help bring about change that will truly benefit them—we have started a charitable organization, the Kurdi Foundation. Helping refugees is Abdullah's one and only dream now. I will do whatever I can to repeat my father's appeal to the world's leaders, to invite all the stakeholders to sit down together and negotiate a peaceful future for my country. Why not? They are mothers and fathers and aunties and uncles just like us. As my father says, "The cure for bad times is patience."

I have to be patient. Syria is my homeland. It's the place where I took root and blossomed. I have to believe that one day it will recover and I will be able to return home. Until then, I will keep dreaming of the day when I can once again walk down the streets of Damascus and breathe in its jasmine-scented air.

Author's Note

I have tried my best to translate select Arabic expressions into English, but there are certain sayings and words for which there is no direct translation. In each case, I have given the most accurate translation possible that still retains the essence of the original phrase, but there may be other variations.

I have also used the particular Arabic dialect that my family speaks in Damascus. Arabic dialects differ widely across the world, so the words and spellings I have used may differ from how they are spoken and written elsewhere.

Acknowledgements

There are so many people I must thank for helping me write this book and share my message. I could not have done any of it alone.

First and foremost, I must thank my parents, who helped me understand how to love and care for others. My *baba* taught me to stand up for those who are struggling. Even when he was enduring his own tragedies, my *baba* always encouraged me to continue with my life and to never lose hope. Without my father, I don't know where I would be right now; my journey is not finished, and I will always need him. My mama was a beautiful, caring mother. She taught us how to be strong and be one family, and she always kept me going. They are both my inspiration in this world.

I will never forget my family members who I've lost. Rehanna, your beautiful smile and happy soul always warmed my heart. Ghalib and Alan, you are angels watching over us. I will miss you each and every day.

Abdullah, your compassion and your work to improve the lives of refugee children everywhere have shown me the true meaning of strength. I could not have told this story without you. Thank you for your courage in turning your tragedy into hope.

To my other sisters and brothers—Mohammad, Maha, Shireen, and Hivron—even though we separated and you are finding a new path forward in your lives, your belief in this book and its message has never wavered. You motivate me to keep going each and every day. I love and miss you all.

Rocco, you have always stood beside me and given me the strength to keep going throughout this process. You have encouraged me to keep speaking for those who are suffering, and you have helped my family at every turn. You understand that we all come from one family and need to be strong together. I am so grateful to have you in my life.

Alan, my son, you are the most good-hearted person I know. Every time we talk, you empower me and remind me not to give up. Your encouragement means the world to me.

To my sister-in-law Anna, thank you for helping me navigate the difficult refugee process and for your tireless efforts to find a way to help my family.

Thank you to everyone who helped with my Group of Five—including Kitt Maitland, Claire Moriarty, and Mike Whittaker—for opening your hearts to my family and for your patience. To Kitt, in particular, thank you for the many months of work during the refugee application process. I could not have done it without you.

Thank you also to Roz Harrington and Rick Speer, Richard Rainy, and Annette Bittermann in Germany. Thank you to all my friends. You know what role each of you has had in my life, and I am so thankful for all of you.

To my editors, Nita Pronovost and Brendan May, thank you for your patience and time. Even though the book was a stressful journey, you always gave me hope and you always listened. I couldn't ask for better editors.

To my agent, Martha Webb, thank you for all your help and hard work in making sure this story is told.

To my writer, Danielle, thank you for capturing my voice, for helping me share my story, and for being so patient at every stage.

Finally, I must thank every person in Canada and across the world who has had the courage to help Syrian refugees or who has raised their voice to demand change for refugees and for the world itself. I don't have enough room here to thank you all by name, but each of you has changed our world for the better. Thank you, everyone.